SECRET
YORK
AN UNUSUAL GUIDE

Isobel Akerman

JONGLEZ PUBLISHING

Travel guides

THE AUTHOR

Isobel Akerman is a writer and researcher who spent her time as a history student at York University exploring the hidden corners of the city. She's worked for small charities and massive companies and has lived in more places than she can remember the names of. At present she's in Cambridge, learning more history and finding more corners.

FOREWORD

We immensely enjoyed writing the *Secret York* guide and hope that, like us, you will continue to discover the unusual, secret and lesser-known facets of this city.

Accompanying the description of some sites, you will find historical information and anecdotes that will let you understand the city in all its complexity.

Secret York also sheds light on the numerous yet overlooked details of places we pass by every day. These details are an invitation to pay more attention to the urban landscape and, more generally, to regard our city with the same curiosity and attention we often feel when travelling ...

Comments on this guide and its contents, as well as information on sites not mentioned, are welcome and will help us to enrich future editions.

Don't hesitate to contact us:
Email: info@jonglezpublishing.com

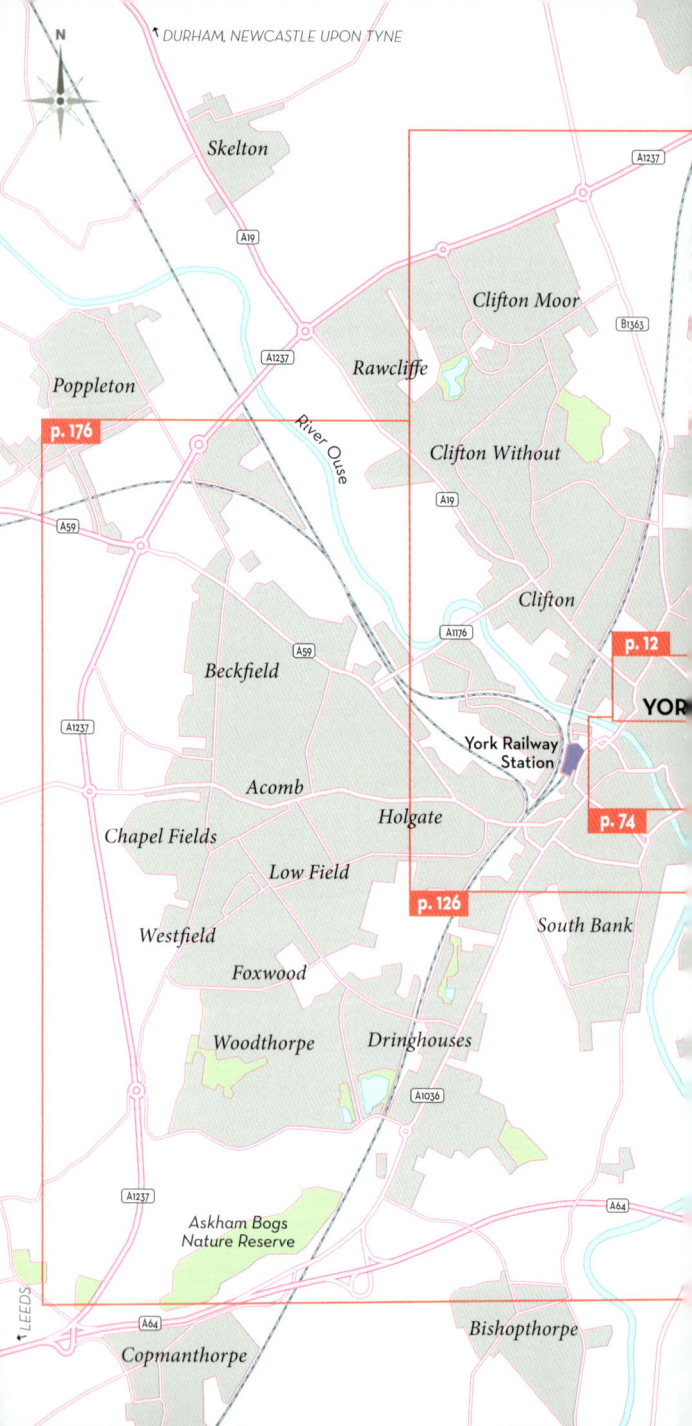

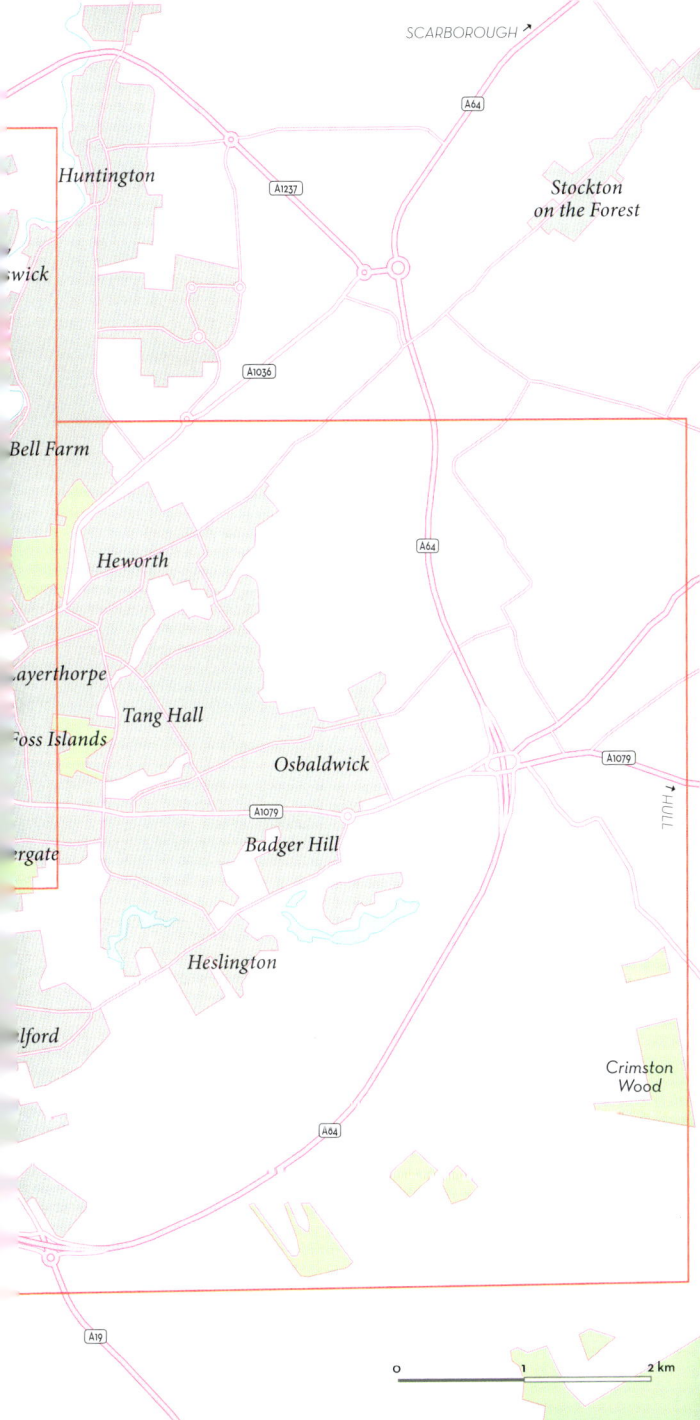

CONTENTS

York Minster

THE CEILING OF THE YORK ART GALLERY	14
THE STATUES OF BOOTHAM BAR	18
THE ROMAN WALL OF BOOTHAM BAR	19
ANGLIAN TOWER	20
DRINKING FOUNTAIN IN MUSEUM GARDENS	22
YORK PHILOSOPHICAL SOCIETY LIBRARY	23
THE VIEW BEHIND THE MULTANGULAR TOWER	24
SNUFFER ON THE RED HOUSE ANTIQUES CENTRE	28
BELL RINGING AT YORK ORATORY	30
THE CROSSED KEYS OF DEAN COURT HOTEL	32
ROYAL MAIL POSTBOX STAMP	34
THE CEREMONY ROOM OF YORK LODGE 236	36
YORK MEDICAL SOCIETY MUSEUM	38
HANGING WOODEN BIBLE	42
THE STONE HOUSE	44
FIRE INSURANCE PLAQUES	46
STATUE OF A NATIVE AMERICAN	48
THE SIREN SCULPTURE	49
THE NAILS OF THE STATUE OF EDWARD II	50
LIBERTY POLICE OFFICE	52
THE MASON'S LOFT	54
CHAPTER HOUSE ROOF	56
OLD PALACE LIBRARY AND ARCHIVE	58
THE HOLY TRINITY CHURCH	60
BEDERN HALL	62
THE COFFIN DROP OF THE GOLDEN SLIPPER PUB	64
THE GLASS CASE OF AN OLD SLIPPER	65
THE MOUSE ON ST WILLIAM'S COLLEGE	65
THE SIGN OF THE GATEWAY TO THE ROMAN FORTRESS	66
THE DUTCH HOUSE	67
THE MERCHANT TAYLORS' HALL	68
JEWBURY PLAQUE	70
ST ANTHONY'S GARDEN	72

Kings Square – Castle

ARUP BUILDING	76
NORTH EASTERN RAILWAY WAR MEMORIAL	78
GEORGE LEEMAN STATUE	80
THE DOORS OF THE YORK GRAND HOTEL BASEMENT	81
CHOLERA BURIAL GROUND	82
JOHN SNOW'S PUMP	83
SNEAK HOLES OF ALL SAINTS CHURCH	84
JACOB'S WELL	86
BISHOPHILL COMMUNITY GARDEN	88
LADY ANNE'S EFFIGY	90
CAT SCULPTURES	92
YORK DRILL AND ARMY MUSEUM	94
PRISONERS' SIGNATURES	96
RAINDALE MILL	98
DICK TURPIN'S FAKE GRAVE	100
LADY PECKETT'S YARD	102
MORRELL YARD	104
CLAY PIPE AT THE BLACK SWAN INN	106
UNITARIAN CHAPEL	108
THE ROCKET IN THE HISCOX BUILDING	110
INSCRIPTION OF THE ANCIENT SOCIETY OF FLORISTS	111
ST ANDREW'S DRILL HALL	112
ROMAN BATH MUSEUM	114
SIGNED BRICKS	116
THE COUNCIL CHAMBER	118
COLUMN OF THE GEORGE INN	120
BETTYS' MIRROR	122
THE MANSION HOUSE CAT	124

Clifton – New Earswick

ALL SAINTS CHURCH	128
NEW EARSWICK	130
AERODROME MEMORIAL	132
YEARSLEY SWIMMING POOL'S INSCRIPTION	134

CONTENTS

ROMAN ROCK	*135*
JOSEPH ROWNTREE THEATRE	*136*
MEMORIAL LIBRARY	*137*
HAXBY ROAD FOOTPATH	*138*
THE BIG BLUE PIPE SCULPTURE	*140*
MANHOLE COVER WITH PULLEYS	*141*
THE DESTRUCTOR	*142*
ICE HOUSE	*143*
BILE BEANS	*144*
PEACE GARDEN	*146*
BOOTHAM PARK HOSPITAL	*148*
BOOTHAM SCHOOL ASSEMBLY HALL	*140*
FORMER ELECTROBUS STATION	*150*
THE RECEPTION OF ST PETER'S SCHOOL	*152*
WOODEN SHUTTERS	*154*
ST MARY'S TOWER	*155*
ST OLAVE'S CHURCHYARD	*156*
SEARCH ENGINE	*158*
THE YORK ZERO POST	*159*
ST PAUL'S SQUARE	*160*
THE PRIESTS' HOLE OF THE SECRET CHAPEL	*162*
THE PROTECTED ODEON SIGN	*163*
BAILE HILL	*164*
BITCHDAUGHTER TOWER	*165*
GAME	*165*
HENRY RICHARDSON'S MEMORIAL	*166*
THE NUNNERY WALL	*168*
THE INSCRIPTION OF THE WATERFRONT HOUSE BAKERY	*170*
FLOOD BOARD	*172*
FOSSGATE BARRIER	*173*
PUBLIC VEGETABLE BED	*174*

Outskirts of York

POPPLETON RAILWAY NURSERY	*178*
THE COLD WAR BUNKER	*180*

HOLGATE WINDMILL	*182*
THE NOSE OF QUEEN VICTORIA'S STATUE	*184*
WHITE ROW	*186*
ST AIDAN'S CHURCH	*187*
BACHELOR HILL	*188*
THE SEVERUS WATER TOWER	*189*
ACOMB WOOD AND MEADOW LOCAL NATURE RESERVE	*190*
ASKHAM BOG	*192*
THE SOLAR SYSTEM CYCLE PATH	*194*
THE PLAGUE STONE	*196*
THE TYBURN STONE	*198*
A SUNSET WALK AT YORK RACECOURSE	*200*
THE STATUE OF TERRY'S CHOCOLATE ORANGE	*202*
MINUTE MEMORIES	*204*
THE ROWNTREE PARK READING CAFÉ	*205*
DISAPPEARING RAILWAY LINES	*206*
PIKEING WELL	*208*
KOHIMA MUSEUM	*210*
THE PLAQUE OF THE GRAVE OF JOSEPH ROWNTREE	*212*
HESLINGTON HALL AND GARDENS	*214*
DRYAD SCULPTURE	*215*
UNIVERSITY OF YORK LAKE	*216*
SIWARD'S HOWE WATER TOWER	*218*
NORMAN TOWER	*220*
VITA YORK	*222*
THE DRAGON STONES	*224*
INNER SPACE STATION SERVICE STATION	*226*
THE TOMB OF MARY WARD	*228*
THE DERWENT VALLEY LIGHT RAILWAY	*230*
ALPHABETICAL INDEX	*232*

York Minster

①	THE CEILING OF THE YORK ART GALLERY	14
②	THE STATUES OF BOOTHAM BAR	18
③	THE ROMAN WALL OF BOOTHAM BAR	19
④	ANGLIAN TOWER	20
⑤	DRINKING FOUNTAIN IN MUSEUM GARDENS	22
⑥	YORK PHILOSOPHICAL SOCIETY LIBRARY	23
⑦	THE VIEW BEHIND THE MULTANGULAR TOWER	24
⑧	SNUFFER ON THE RED HOUSE ANTIQUES CENTRE	28
⑨	BELL RINGING AT YORK ORATORY	30
⑩	THE CROSSED KEYS OF DEAN COURT HOTEL	32
⑪	ROYAL MAIL POSTBOX STAMP	34
⑫	THE CEREMONY ROOM OF YORK LODGE 236	36
⑬	YORK MEDICAL SOCIETY MUSEUM	38
⑭	HANGING WOODEN BIBLE	42
⑮	THE STONE HOUSE	44
⑯	FIRE INSURANCE PLAQUES	46
⑰	STATUE OF A NATIVE AMERICAN	48

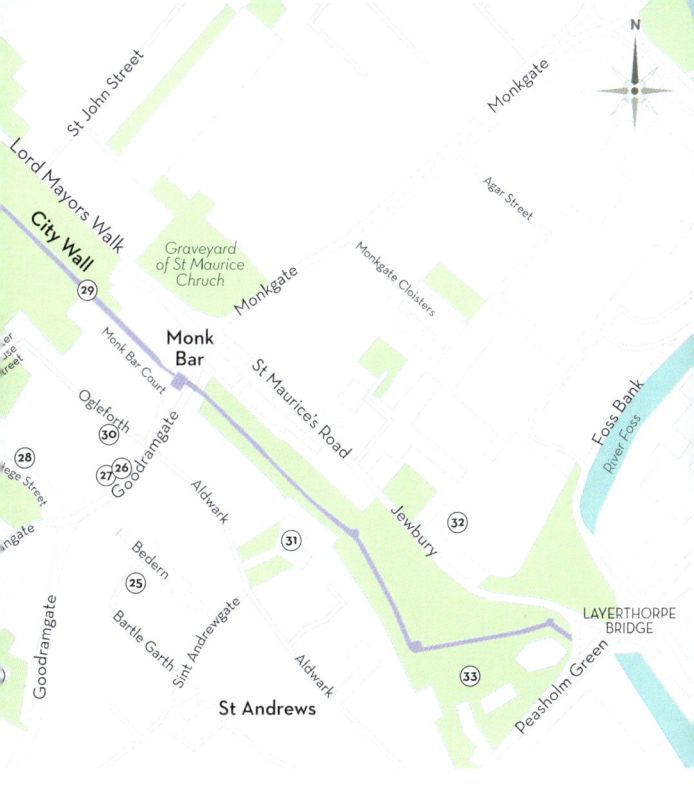

⑱ THE SIREN SCULPTURE	49
⑲ THE NAILS OF THE STATUE OF EDWARD II	50
⑳ LIBERTY POLICE OFFICE	52
㉑ THE MASON'S LOFT	54
㉒ CHAPTER HOUSE ROOF	56
㉓ OLD PALACE LIBRARY AND ARCHIVE	58
㉔ THE HOLY TRINITY CHURCH	60
㉕ BEDERN HALL	62
㉖ THE COFFIN DROP OF THE GOLDEN SLIPPER PUB	64
㉗ THE GLASS CASE OF AN OLD SLIPPER	65
㉘ THE MOUSE ON ST WILLIAM'S COLLEGE	65
㉙ THE SIGN OF THE GATEWAY TO THE ROMAN FORTRESS	66
㉚ THE DUTCH HOUSE	67
㉛ THE MERCHANT TAYLORS' HALL	68
㉜ JEWBURY PLAQUE	70
㉝ ST ANTHONY'S GARDEN	72

THE CEILING OF THE YORK ART GALLERY

A ceiling which had been hiding for 70 years

Exhibition Square, YO1 7EW
yorkartgallery.org.uk
Wednesday–Sunday 11am–4pm
All tickets include access to the permanent collection as well as all special exhibitions

Considering the uninviting façade of the York Art Gallery, its upstairs floors – which are decked out in bright ceramics and postmodern exhibits – are a pleasant surprise. Aside from the impressive art pieces displayed along the walls, the beautiful and ornate ceiling of the first-floor gallery is a hidden gem in itself.

For years, this ceiling was concealed behind a fake roof which was put up in the 1940s so that the curators could control the environment of their exhibits. The unveiling of the original ceiling and the new 15-metre mezzanine space is the product of an £8m refurbishment in 2013, which brought the old Victorian art gallery into the 21st century. The refurbishment removed the fake roof and revealed the spectacular ceiling which had been hiding behind it for 70 years.

After starting the journey through the gallery with the traditional and predictable portraits and landscapes, the mezzanine offers an incredible variety of British ceramics – the largest collection to be found anywhere in the world. With its skylights and windows, the space is too bright to preserve sensitive paintings, but is perfect for the mixture of collages, sculptures and pottery dating all the way back to pre-history that make up the changing exhibitions curated by the Centre of Ceramic Art.

The Centre of Ceramic Art was also created when the Art Gallery re-opened a few years ago. With their new permanent space for exhibitions and plans to create a comprehensive digital archive, the Centre is continuing their work in promoting ceramics as a crucial and specialist branch of British Modernist Art.

'The first modern lesbian'

At Exhibition Square, King's Manor is a collection of beautiful old buildings which now forms part of the University of York's campus. If the downstairs dining rooms are well known for hosting numerous kings on their historic visits to the city, it was in the attics of the Manor House Boarding School that a far more secret liaison took place: this was where Anne Lister, often referred to as 'the first modern lesbian', had her first love affair with schoolmate Eliza Reine.

Anne came from a good background – she was the daughter of a wealthy merchant and lived on a huge estate in Halifax, but due to several tragic events that led to the deaths of all four of her brothers, she became the sole heir to the estate. Initially home-schooled, her high intelligence became apparent very quickly, and at 15 she was sent away to receive a formal education at Manor House School.

Although always flirtatious, Anne had never had a serious relationship before going to King's Manor. Described as a 'tomboy', she was not shy about pursuing romantic relationships. Although male homosexuality was illegal at this time, it never occurred to the law makers to comment explicitly on female activities. When she and Eliza were banished to the attic room (which they nicknamed 'the Slope') as part of an attempted punishment, she initiated an intense love affair that started a chain of notorious dalliances and an independent sexual identity.

Both girls kept diaries where their love affair was defined by intimate companionship: they spoke in code, bought each other gifts and referred to each other as 'husband'. Eliza never wavered in her affection, but Anne pursued several other relationships upon leaving King's Manor. Eliza was tragically declared insane after having to come to terms with unrequited love, while Anne ended up living openly on her family estate with an heiress called Ann Walker. A blue plaque can be found outside the Holy Trinity Church which commemorates the location of Lister and Walker's spiritual marriage.

Anne's diaries have been translated and published – it must have been quite an endeavour to decipher the codes and language of a lovestruck teenager – and her life became the inspiration for the BBC Drama *Gentleman Jack*. A few of the scenes in the production were filmed in the buildings of York, so keep your eye out when watching.

YORK CIVIC TRUST
Anne Lister
1791 - 1840
of Shibden Hall, Halifax
Lesbian and Diarist;
took sacrament here to seal her
union with Ann Walker
Easter 1834

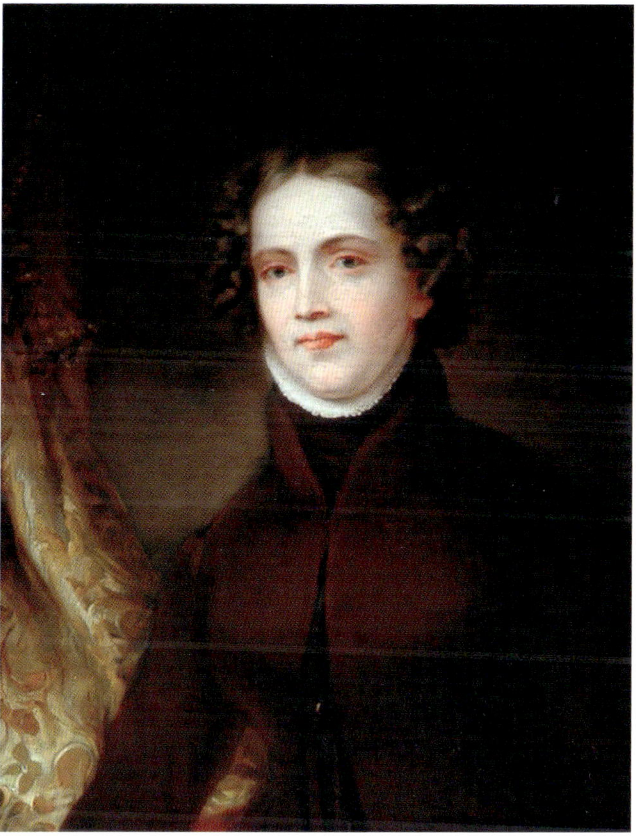

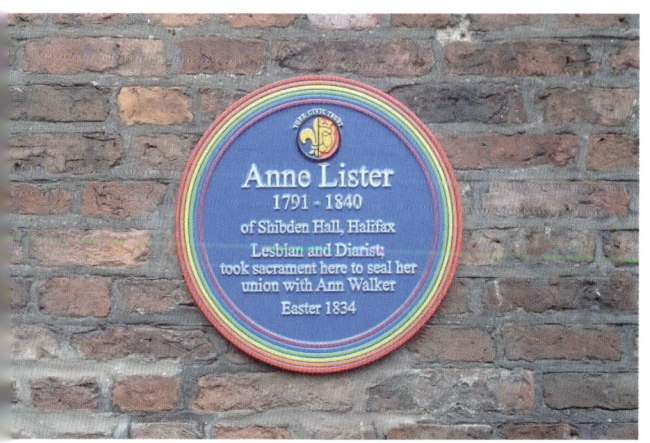

THE STATUES OF BOOTHAM BAR ②

The protectors of York

2–4 High Petergate, York YO1 7EH

At the top of Bootham Bar are three statues looking out towards the horizon, steadfastly waiting in case of attack from the North. The symbolic statues represent the three crucial points of defence for the city: the knight who fights the invaders, the mason who builds the walls, and the mayor who holds the key.

There has been a fortress on this spot since Roman times, but the statues themselves are 19th-century remakes of the 14th-century originals. Extra defences were put in place after a war with Scotland led to Yorkshire being pillaged by the Scottish armies. In an attempt to fight them off, a Yorkshire army was formed from a brave but inexperienced and ill-equipped military force comprised of local volunteers – it even included clerics, priests and monks. The fortress has several effective defences built into the design. One is the portcullis, (a huge heavy gate) which can be seen inside the bar. Even in more peaceful times there

was an effort to keep the Scots out. A passive-aggressive door knocker was added to the entrance of the bar, exclusively forcing any Scotsman to knock and request permission before entering the city. The knocker has since been removed and the Scots can come and go as they like. However, the law that allowed a Yorkshireman to shoot a Scotsman with a bow and arrow was only made illegal with the enactment of the Human Rights Act in 1998.

NEARBY
The Roman wall of Bootham Bar ③
Bootham Bar Gateway, Exhibition Square, YO1 7EW
Next door to Bootham Bar, almost part of the wall itself, is a little café which opened in 2015. The café sat on top of a large section of the original Roman wall which had been protected by a concrete barrier in the early 20th century. This barrier was uncovered during construction. The wall reveals the original street level of the city over 2,000 years ago when it was the legionary fortress of Eboracum. It can now be admired through a glass floor.

ANGLIAN TOWER

Britain's last Anglo-Saxon building?

Museum Gardens, Museum Street, YO1 7FR
Daily 9am–6pm
Accessible via the museum gardens or around the York Explore side gate

Behind the back of York Library, and a little way along the remains of the old walls, is a small stone building. Because it is so well hidden not many people know about this little gem, but it has been described as the most interesting building in the entire country by the archaeological organisation Historic UK.

This cramped stone room attached to the York Walls was thought to be the only surviving secular building from the Anglo-Saxon period (from the 5th century until the Battle of Hastings in 1066). Although we are spoilt with the number of Anglo-Saxon churches still standing, every other type of building from this era throughout the whole of Europe has been destroyed, and this tower was thought to have been the last one to endure. However, because the masons used freshly quarried oolitic limestone rather than re-used Roman bricks, scholars now believe that the tower is in fact late Roman or 'sub-Roman' rather than Anglo-Saxon. Although archaeologists and historians are getting closer to the truth of the tower, origin dates vary from anywhere between 300 AD and 700 AD, and its true history remains a mystery.

The original purpose of the tower is also an intriguing question. Only the ground floor room of the tower survives, but archaeologists consider this exciting enough: with this, they can make a few educated guesses as to what the structure was used for. Being built into what would have been the original Roman wall, it may have been used as a watchtower, or an archery platform, or merely a walkthrough for people to access the walls.

Unfortunately, without the rest of the tower there's no way to know for sure. It became buried under Danish ramparts around 900 AD following the Viking invasion of England, and stayed hidden for hundreds of years. The remains were discovered by accident in 1839 when a team of workmen were building a tunnel nearby, although the site was only properly excavated in the 1960s.

DRINKING FOUNTAIN IN MUSEUM GARDENS

The first public drinking fountain in York

Museum Gardens, Museum Street, YO1 7FR
yorkmuseumgardens.co.uk
Daily 9am–6pm

The public drinking fountain, although a relatively simple idea, was one of the health miracles of the 19th century. In reaction to large numbers of people dying from waterborne diseases, fountains started appearing around the country in an attempt to persuade the public to stop drinking polluted river-water, water from stagnant wells, or water alternatives (primarily beer). The drinking fountain outside the Museum Gardens was the first to be erected in York – it was designed by sculptor and mason Job Cole, and donated to the city in 1880 by Henry Cowling, a local solicitor.

As well as health and safety motivations, the fountain demonstrated a certain type of hydro-philanthropy of which the Victorians were huge fans. Following Jon Snow's discovery that cholera was transmitted through dirty water (see *Secret London – an unusual guide* from the same publisher), the act of charitable water-giving demonstrated both a generous nature and scientific intellect. Thus, this fountain was not just to protect health, but was also intended to showcase the modernisation of the city and concern for public welfare. Things moved on relatively quickly, however, and soon individuals began to gain access to clean water in their homes, with public fountains becoming less important: this particular fountain has been out of use for years, and people have probably not even noticed.

Despite not working anymore, the fountain is still a beautiful piece of sculpture. It has two almost identical faces: one looking out at the street, and the other into Museum Gardens' ... perhaps York Philosophical Society (who owned the gardens when the fountain was erected) did not want to share a drinking cup with the general public. The only difference between the two is that the Museum Gardens' side has the sign of St Peter (see page 32), and the public side has the coat of arms of the City of York.

NEARBY
York Philosophical Society Library

The Lodge, Museum Gardens, York YO1 7DR
ypsyork.org
See website for opening hours for non-members

On the other side of the gate to the fountain is a small building guarding the entrance to the Museum Gardens. The library of the York Philosophical Society is only open to members or by private appointment, and holds a wealth of knowledge on local aspects of York, in particular archaeology, geology and natural history. Although access to the library is restricted, the museum and shop on the ground floor are open to the public.

THE VIEW BEHIND THE MULTANGULAR TOWER

The most striking defensive part of the original Roman fortress

Museum Street, YO1 7FR
Daily 9am–6pm

In the peaceful Museum Gardens is an ostentatious structure called the Multangular Tower: it is the most striking defensive part of the original Roman fortress, and one of the more recognisable sections of the wall. Although the exterior is well known, many people don't realise that you can sneak through a path to the left and look behind the tower. It is this perspective that demonstrates what a feat of Roman engineering the tower must have been in its heyday.

The large circular tower would have been around 10 metres high and was designed to protrude out from the fortress, rather than sit behind it. This was a new technique, which meant archers could fire sideways on invaders trying to clamber over the walls into the city. There were originally eight of these towers throughout the city, but the multangular tower is the only one left.

The tower is made up of different types of stones which have been assembled over the centuries. The small Roman stones are at the very bottom, with the larger medieval ones built on top. The Romans used a square stone called the *saxa quadrata* which was made to look like modern brick – some even have fake vertical lines carved into them to make the stones appear more even. These stones were then held together by a layer of red tiles that runs around the structure.

Also displayed in this area are Roman coffins that have been found around and outside the city during excavations. They are made of millstone grit, which explains how they have survived intact for so long – at some point, one has even been used as a horse trough!

Boundary Stones

To suggest stones for the project contact info@yorkcivictrust.co.uk
Boundary stones have been used for centuries to mark ownership, location, civic functions, or measurement of land. York has over 90 boundary stones hidden around the city, but some are almost impossible to find without being given the exact co-ordinates. And even if you're standing on top of one, many of these markers are so worn down, with the inscriptions so faded or covered by vegetation, that you would never know they had once demarcated something like the boundary of someone's land, the border between two parishes, or a sign telling travellers from afar that they were nearing the entrance to the city. Because of their inconspicuousness, the heritage stones are often at risk of being thrown away or built over. Luckily, a York Civic Trust project is underway to find out more about these stones and discover their locations. Volunteers have been venturing out into all sorts of corners of the wider city limits to try and find the markers and uncover their histories. This is proving fairly difficult, however. One stone, for example, found at the end Station Road in Upper Poppleton, would seem to be the marker between two districts (Upper Poppleton and Nether Poppleton) – however, the archival research question as to whether the two parishes ever met at this point is yet to be answered …

Historic Street Signs

Another project led by the Civic Trust is the renovation of the faded historic street signs that still decorate the city's roads and snickleways. The names of York's streets and alleyways have changed over the centuries, and from 1782 York began to put up official signs with street names on them, often to denote the activities that went on. Nunnery Lane, for example, was formerly called Baggergate Lane in medieval times due to its association with bag making.

Grape Lane was once Grope Lane, denoting the ladies of the night that could be propositioned there.

The old street signs that give clues to these earlier activities are part of York's history. Many were hand-carved into stone blocks by specialist craftsmen using a particular York-specific font, before the style moved to cast iron or wooden signs which are now more common. Working with sign writer Phil Paylor, the York Civic Trust are ensuring that these older, worn-out signs are restored using the original 18th-century process of traditional signwriting.

SNUFFER ON THE RED HOUSE ANTIQUES CENTRE

⑧

Extinguishing the light

1 Duncombe Place, YO1 7ED
antiques-atlas.com/theredhouseantiquescentre

Attached to the outside wall of The Red House Antiques Centre is an 18th-century antique that is just as interesting as any of the objects

inside. This black cast-iron cone is called a 'snuffer' which, although completely useless nowadays, was of paramount importance a few hundred years ago when the house was built. Before the introduction of modern streetlighting, when it was dark outside the upper classes would employ 'link-men' to walk in front of them holding burning torches, lighting their way as they travelled about the city. This was especially important in York, where the tiny alleyways and overhanging houses presented petty thieves with numerous after-dark opportunities. Once their clients were safely home, the link-men would use the snuffers to extinguish their torches and be on their way.

For a few generations, The Red House was home to the wealthier citizens of York. Built as the town residence for Sir William Robinson, Lord Mayor of the city and Member of Parliament, it later became the home of Dr John Burton, who was the inspiration for the infamous character of Dr Slop in *The Life and Opinions of Tristam Shandy, Gentleman* by Lawrence Sterne, the son of the then archbishop of York. Given Dr Slop's general medical incompetence (in 2011 he was voted as one of the 'best bad doctors of literature'), the relationship between Mr Sterne and Dr Burton was clearly not close. The building has since passed into various hands and is now owned by the York Conservation Trust. It has been formally protected by the Royal Commission on the Ancient and Historical Monuments of England due to its significance in illustrating the past lives of the people of York.

NEARBY
Boot scrapers

Outside The Red House, as well as the snuffer, you will also see two boot scrapers, one on either side of the entrance. The roads of York were often filthy with mud, dirt and worse (the contents of chamber pots were usually emptied directly onto the street): these boot scrapers were essential for removing the muck that accumulated on people's shoes.

Link-men were sometimes referred to as 'moon cursers' because if the moon shone brightly enough then they were out of a job.

Other snuffers in York
There are actually three examples of this unusual piece of street furniture in York: one here, one on Gillygate and one outside the Guy Fawkes Pub.

BELL RINGING AT YORK ORATORY

⑨

Pealing the bells

The Oratory Church of St Wilfrid, Duncombe Place, YO1 7EF
Bell ringing by appointment only, contact tower@yorkoratory.com

There are over 30 regular volunteers who make up the band of bell ringers at the York Oratory, and although most of the volunteers have a qualification from the Association of Ringing Teachers, any novice, amateur, or pro can request to join them in the bell tower to have a go at 'ringing the changes'. Before heading up the 54 steps to the ringing room, you should know not to ask whether you can play any of your favourite church melodies. The ten pealing bells of the York Oratory are designed to play a suite of mathematical permeations, rather than the classics. Permeations are the patterns that can be woven between the notes of the bells – the ringers peal them with an accuracy of about 1/20th of a second in order to create an even rhythm.

Designed in a circle around the tiny tower room, all the bells are in the key of F and are placed in order of size, each getting lower in pitch as they become larger (the largest being the Tenor at 936 kg, about the weight of a small car). It needs teamwork, strength and precision, but when it all goes right, the sounds they produce are magical.

Aside from the bells, another interesting feature of the bell-ringing room is the sole stained-glass window built into the wall, a heartfelt memorial to one of the founding members of the ringers.

Competition of angles

The churches of York have occasionally competed against each other for the best spot on York's landscape – St Wilfrid versus the Minster is one of the best examples. St Wilfrid's tower was deliberately designed to make the church look bigger than the York Minster Cathedral if you walk up Museum Street from the river. This trick of perspective has given rise to a number of confusing but entertaining photographs which distort the size of both buildings.

THE CROSSED KEYS
OF DEAN COURT HOTEL

The symbol of a formal territory which was free from the jurisdiction of the Lord Mayor

Duncombe Place, YO1 7EF

YORK MINSTER

Hidden in the brickwork of the Dean Court Hotel, high on the wall that faces the York Minster Cathedral, is the symbol of St Peter: the two crossed keys that open the gates to heaven.

The keys were included in the Victorian structure when it was designed in 1865 by the renowned York architects J.B. & W. Atkinson. Initially built for members of the York Minster Clergy, the building was converted into a hotel in the early part of the 20th century.

Even with the religious origins of the building, it still seems an unusual symbol to feature on the side of a house. The reason that the keys can be seen on the hotel here lies in its location: on the corner of High Petergate in the shadow of the Cathedral.

In the 13th century this area was given to the archbishop of York as part of a formal territory which was free from the jurisdiction of the lord mayor. It acted as a 'city within a city', with its own laws, courts, officers, taxes, prisons and gallows – all overseen by the archbishop. Today it could broadly be compared to Vatican City in Rome, which falls under the pope's authority.

The territory was named *The Liberty of St Peter* after the Cathedral's official title *The Cathedral Metropolitical Church of St Peter in York* and the cross keys of St Peter was its symbol.

For over 600 years there were ongoing clashes between the Liberty of St Peter and the civic authorities over taxes, jurisdiction and power until 1839 when the entire area within the City Walls came under the Lord Mayor's rule.

The Liberty of St Peter is no more but its symbol still appears noticeably in numerous places around York, echoing the memory of the bygone city. Once you start looking, you'll start seeing it everywhere: on walls, bridges, carvings, shop signs, pub names and business logos.

ROYAL MAIL POSTBOX STAMP

50 years of Special Stamps

Duncombe Place, YO1 7DX
shop.royalmail.com/special-stamp-issues

The postbox on Duncombe place looks like your standard, run-of-the-mill Royal Mail postbox. But the plaque attached to it – which is decorated with a picture of York Minster – makes a very special postbox, completely one of a kind.

This image of York Minster is one of the most popular features in the Royal Mail's 'Special Stamps' collection which started in 1965. To celebrate the 50th anniversary of this collection in 2015, 50 of these special stamps were made into plaques and attached to postboxes around the country.

Before the Special Collection began, all British stamps depicted the profile of the reigning monarch. However, following the death of Winston Churchill in January 1965, the postmaster general at the time decided to adapt tradition and put Mr Churchill's recognisable face (minus the cigar) front and centre. The stamp was so popular that the Royal Mail continued issuing new stamp themes, leading to an incredible variety of images, including *Star Wars*, The Beatles, and *Thomas the Tank Engine*, all of which are taken to the Queen to approve before being printed.

In total, the Special Stamp Collection now numbers over 2,000 individual stamps depicting images from over 2,000 years of British life and history. York has appeared in many of these prints, including portraits of the kings and queens of the medieval House of York, the Yorkist victory over the Lancastrians in the Battle of Tewkesbury and a celebration of the city's 1900th anniversary. But it is the 1969 stamp of York Minster designed by Peter Gauld which made the top 50 and found its place on the Duncombe Place postbox.

From green to red ...

Created in 1840 by a teacher called Rowland Hill, the 'Penny Black' was the first stamp to appear in Britain. The idea of sending letters at a standard prepaid price was a revolutionary change: before this it was a complicated system based on a price-per-sheet with differing costs depending on which city you were in. The iconic red postbox came 12 years later in 1852, and was designed by Anthony Trollope, who as well as being a famous author also worked for the post office. Initially painted green to blend into its surroundings, the pillars became too difficult to find, so they were changed to red in order to be more easily identified and reduce the stress of sending letters.

THE CEREMONY ROOM OF YORK LODGE 236

Secret temple

Masonic Hall, YO1 7DX
To arrange a visit, contact yorklodge236@gmail.com

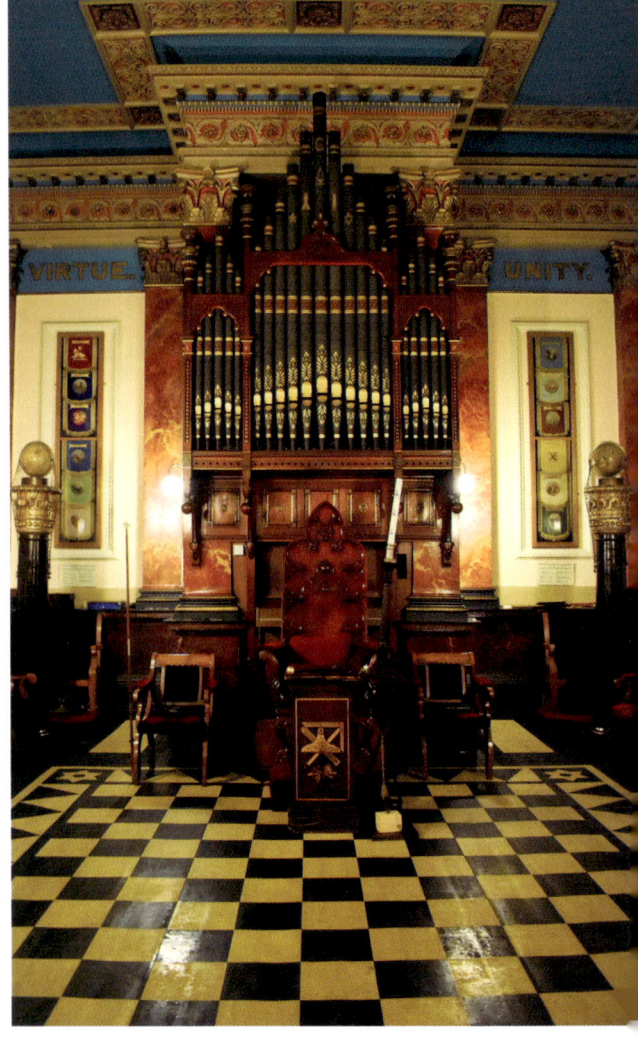

Despite their reputation for being secretive, the Freemasons have recently embarked on a national public relations campaign to become slightly more transparent, and so the doors to the ceremony room of York Lodge 236 have finally been opened to the public.

The Freemasons of York have operated inside the Gothic walls of the Masonic Hall since 1863 when it was purpose built as a base for the society. With its golden thrones, high pillars and Masonry symbols, the central ceremony room is referred to as 'The Temple'.

Through a ritual that goes back hundreds of years, after an individual has requested to join, all members are called to ballot for any new candidate or those joining from another Lodge. A small hook on the ceremony room entrance door is locked from the outside by the Tyler (guard) and each member casts their vote: the result must be unanimous before any new member is admitted. When the society was first officially formalised in Britain in the 1700s, a new recruit could only join when they had become a 'master' of their craft. Eventually anyone could request to join as long as they had a recommendation from an existing member. Politicians, philanthropists, royalty, businessmen and many more, created an international network of 'brothers' who were recognisable to each other through secret handshakes and particular turns of phrase.

Despite declining membership, the society continues. It is the second largest donator to charity in the country, and due to the increasingly liberal definitions of their core teachings of brotherly love, relief and truth, there are now no religious restrictions to membership.

Women in the fraternity

Behind a vault door in the library of York Lodge 236 are ancient society manuscripts known as the 'York Rolls' which can be taken out to view by special request. Roll number four has been the basis of controversy for many years. When defining the rituals for joining the society, it states '... he or she that is to be made a Mason', thereby seemingly admitting women into the fraternity, but it has been described by most members as a mistake.

YORK MEDICAL SOCIETY MUSEUM

⑬

A lecture hall, a bespoke museum, a medical library and a secret garden ...

23 Stonegate, YO1 8AW
yorkmedsoc.org
Pre-booked tours only, see website for details

Marking the location of York Medical Society, a small sign on the gates of 23 Stonegate is the only indication that the alleyway behind the black bars leads anywhere in particular. Yet, despite the nondescript entrance, hidden through the narrow courtyard and within the building is a lecture hall, a bespoke museum, a medical library and a secret garden with a private view of the Minster. York Medical Society have been practising in the city for almost 200 years with the purpose of 'promoting and diffusing medical knowledge'. In 1915 they settled in Stonegate, in an old Elizabethan house (now owned by the York Conservation Trust) that has the oldest rainwater head in York, sitting on top of the arched entrance (dated 1590). The Society now has about 300 members and is open to anyone on the General Medical Council register, but also to anyone who books a tour on their website.

The mini museum is found inside and the objects that are now displayed in glass cabinets have been accumulating over the years through donations from different members. There is now an impressive array of historic medical curiosities, including old operating kits, glass eyewear, and historic amputation equipment. Outside, in the Medical Society's private garden, there are not any medicinal plants growing, but the space is so calm and full of colour that it must be good for your health: the architect who worked on a restoration of the building in the 1970s described it as a 'haven of peace' in the heart of the city.

Regional medical societies first appeared in England in the 19th century when local physicians and surgeons began to share and expand their knowledge by gathering to discuss the latest ideas and practices. Before moving to its current headquarters, York Medical Society had difficulty finding a permanent home. It met sporadically in the old York Dispensary or in rented rooms dotted around the city, which did not help attendance. The previous owner of the house before the society moved in was Dr Tempest Anderson, a renowned 19th century scientist and volcanologist who has a whole room dedicated to his work in the Society's headquarters, as well as a commemorative plaque hanging up outside the entrance.

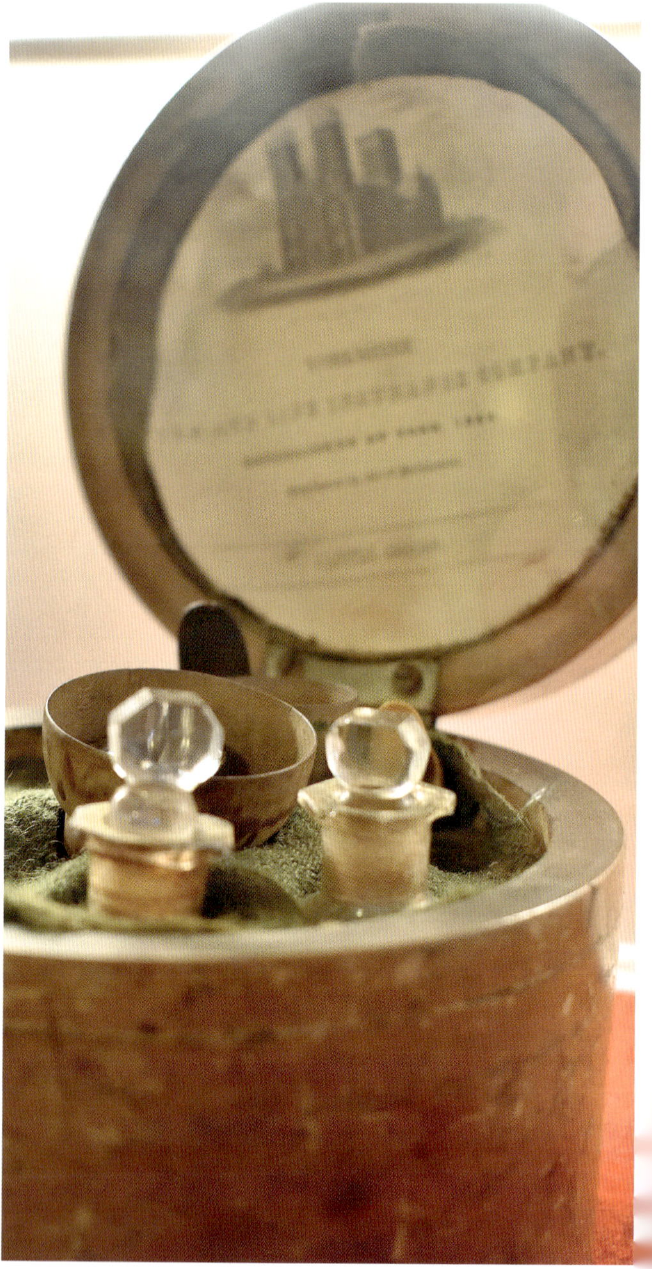

Pulsometer

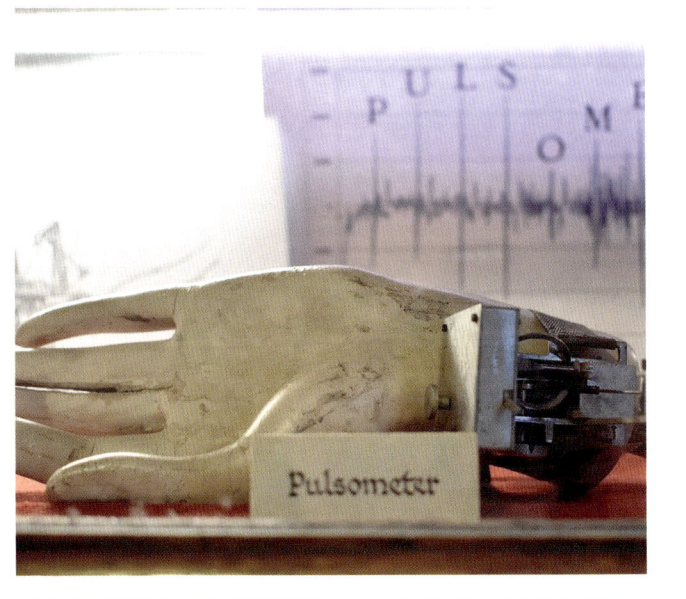

Bougies

HANGING WOODEN BIBLE

The vestige of a former renowned bookshop

35 Stonegate, YO1 8AW

Generally, retail shops do not present you with religious themes as soon as you step through the door. But in York, everything was once something else: in the 1600s, the shop at 35 Stonegate used to be a renowned bookshop called The Sign of the Bible. A wooden Bible was hung over the door to advertise the business and one still hangs there today, slightly out of place for a contemporary shop.

Opened in 1682, The Sign of the Bible soon became the most popular bookshop and printer in the city. It also functioned as one of the first 'circulating libraries', which allowed subscribers to rent books for an annual fee, triggering the mass culture of reading by allowing more people access to new books.

The elaborately decorated design of the building (which you can see sticks out like an embellished sore thumb on the old-fashioned Stonegate street) is thanks to the 19th-century owner, John Warde Knowles. A headstrong young man, John Knowles was a glass painter by trade who, as well as re-designing the interior and adding a glass workshop at the rear, also changed the entire frontage of his home to suit his extravagant tastes, much to the dismay of neighbouring businesses.

His stained-glass windows are still there to admire as you shop.

THE STONE HOUSE

The oldest home in York

48–50 Stonegate, YO1 6AS
Usually accessible to view at any reasonable time

Being the oldest house in a city overflowing with old houses is certainly something to brag about, but this important historic building is nonetheless surprisingly difficult to find. It is tucked away behind the dark-wooden door of No. 52A on the busy street of

Stonegate: look out for the small sign above the entrance that reads 'to the remains of the XII century house'. Through the narrow archway that lies behind this door, you will find the open courtyard, crumbling stone walls and solitary window that make up the remains of York's oldest surviving domestic home.

The original house was constructed in the late 12th century, during a period when stone was an expensive and seldom-used material. This large stone house would therefore have been unusual, standing out from the neighbouring timbered houses as an impressive display of its owner's wealth and status.

The use of stone might initially suggest that this was a religious or public building; however, there are a number of features discovered by archaeologists that mark the site out as a domestic residence, such as the remains of a rare indoor medieval toilet called a *garderobe*, and a shutter-hinge for timber shutters which can still be seen attached to the arched window.

Very little is known about the inhabitants of this house during its first 200 years, but what has provided some insight into its beginnings are the similarities that can be found to the 'Norman House' in the city of Lincoln – about 80 miles away from York. That house was built for Aaron of Lincoln, a wealthy Jewish financier. The windows of both Norman houses are identical, and it is likely that they were built at the same time by the closely linked Jewish communities in each city.

The site went on to become a home to the York Minster clergy in the 15th century and remained so for over 400 years. Subsequent development of the area resulted in more and more buildings encroaching on the land, until eventually all trace of the original house disappeared. The stone walls were rediscovered when renovations took place on the site in 1939.

FIRE INSURANCE PLAQUES
The first fire cover

27 and the building that was the former site of 31 High Petergate, YO1 7HP

If your house was burning down it would be fairly frustrating if, before tackling the blaze, the fire brigade first wanted to establish whether or not you had fire insurance. But in the past many fire brigades were owned by private fire insurance firms and would only extinguish the fires of houses that were insured by their company.

To make things easier, the insurance companies would attach plaques with their company's logo onto the walls of customers' houses as proof of insurance, so there would be no need to check. These little plaques are now rare, but not unheard of. In York, where old houses are preserved and protected, two of these logos can still be spotted.

The plaque outside 27 High Petergate represents the Sun Fire Insurance company which was set up in 1710 and continues today as the Royal and Sun Alliance. The plaque would have been one of the first of its kind – it consists of the emblem of the company (a sun with human features) and the individual policy number, so as to identify any claim made.

Further along at what was formerly No. 31 High Petergate is another example made in the early 1800s – it is the logo of County Fire Insurance, depicting Britannia and the royal coat of arms. Note that this plaque, being more modern than the Sun Insurance sign, does not have a policy number engraved on it.

As time went on, these plaques became more of a marketing ploy than a useful tool of identification, until eventually they lost all purpose other than being objects of curiosity.

The main problem that the companies faced was that of uncontrolled blazes – fires spread from house to house, indiscriminately burning down both the insured and uninsured houses. Eventually, with increasing numbers of private fire brigades, it was decided it would be more efficient to bring everything under local government control – the Public Fire Service was born and all homes came under its protection.

> The concept of fire insurance only began in England after the Great Fire of London in 1666, which left hundreds of people homeless, jobless and in huge amounts of debt. The companies were set up much like insurers of today, taking payments from customers and paying for the damage to houses if disaster were to strike.

STATUE
OF A NATIVE AMERICAN

The cigar-store figure

74A Low Petergate
York YO1 7HZ

Outside 76 Low Petergate is a wooden statue caricaturing the Native American of 17th-century imagination.

Featuring cultural stereotypes of the time such as headdresses, feathers representing tobacco leaves and nakedness, this statue was called a 'cigar-store Indian' or 'Virginian': it was used to advertise cigars because tobacco plants were found in the Americas.

In an age of illiteracy, statues such as this one were commonly found outside tobacconist shops to show people what the stores sold inside.

NEARBY
The siren sculpture
13 Stonegate, YO1 8AN

A little way down from the Stonegate Devil is another ancient figure overlooking the busy street. Often mistaken for a mermaid, the wooden statue attached to the corner of No. 13 Stonegate is actually a siren, a mythical being that is half-woman, half-bird. This particular siren was made in the 17th century and acted as the figurehead for a ship. Although we don't know how she came to be in York, the statue has been attached to this building for hundreds of years; she was fully restored by a local master woodcarver in 1978 on behalf of the York Civic Trust.

THE NAILS OF THE STATUE OF EDWARD II

The bored king

York Minster Choir Screen
York Minster, 8 Minster Yard, YO1 7HL
yorkminster.org
Monday–Saturday 9.30am–4pm, Sunday 12.45pm–2.30pm
For admission prices and booking, see website

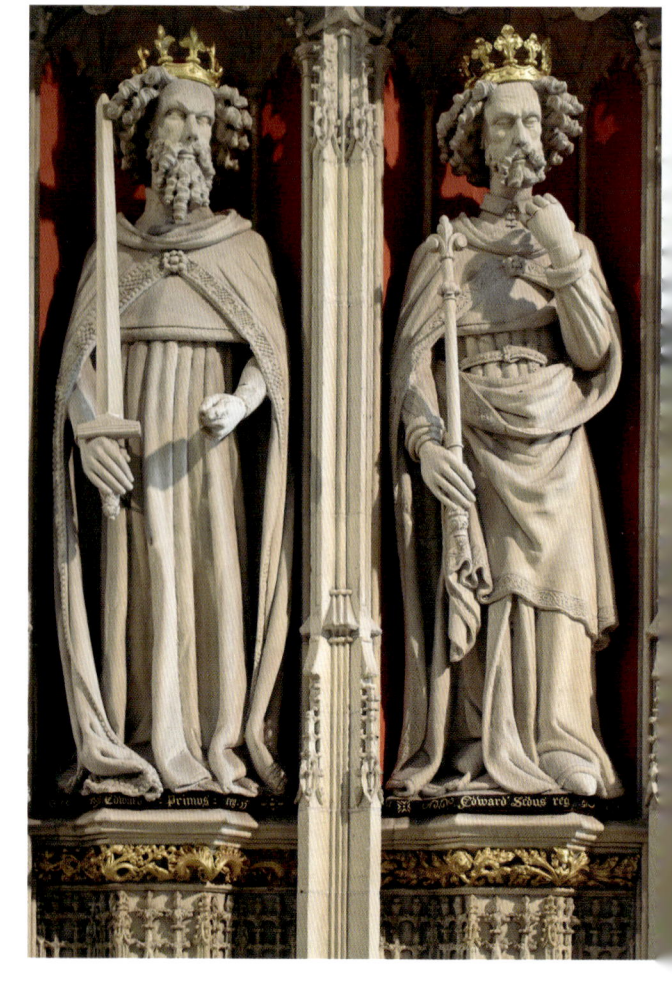

YORK MINSTER

The Minster's ornate choir screen presents beautifully carved depictions of several English kings, starting with William the Conqueror and ending with Henry VI. Each almost life-sized statue is a charming depiction of the real thing, and their individual personalities are represented through period fashions, distinctive details and recognisable facial features chosen by the sculptor, Willian Hyndeley.

The screen was commissioned by Henry V around 1420, but Hyndeley did not finish it until Henry VI had ascended the throne, which is why there are seven kings on one side and eight on the other, with the young King Henry VI squeezed onto the end.

Medieval humour is a constant feature in the carvings of York Minster and the choir screen is no exception. At first glance it might seem like a proud line of England's royalty but there is one king who has been given a bit of a hard time. Prowess in war was the defining feature of a 'good king' in medieval England and yet, while most of these kings have been carved holding a sword in preparation for a fight, Edward II stands on his pedestal swordless, more preoccupied with examining his nails than winning any wars.

By all accounts Edward was not a great soldier. During his reign (1307–1327) he had some crushing defeats on the battlefield – most famously his humiliating failure in the battle of Bannockburn against Scotland. The English people were not happy with their less-than-ideal military leader, which is why he is shown to be an oblivious bystander while his father stands disapprovingly next to him.

LIBERTY POLICE OFFICE

One of the very few cathedral police forces in the world

York Minster, 8 Minster Yard, YO1 7HL
yorkminster.org
Monday–Saturday 9.30am–4pm, Sunday 12.45pm–2.30pm
For admission prices and booking, see website

Past the north transept in York Minster, opposite the choir, there are two truncheons mounted on a wooden plaque, looking rather out of place in a cathedral. These batons signpost the office of the Minster Police force. The existence of a cathedral police force is a surprise to most visitors. In fact, there are only five others in the world: Canterbury, Liverpool, Chester, St Peter's Basilica (Rome) and the Washington National Cathedral.

The Minster Police were assigned to protect the Liberty of St Peter, the area of land under the authority of the archbishop of York in the 13th century. The Liberty had a separate jurisdiction from the City Police and so the archbishop needed constables to enforce the rule of law within his remit. This unit was formed so long ago that it pre-dates the national Metropolitan Police Force by 600 years: it could in fact be the oldest police body still in existence.

The Minster Police have mostly spent their time overseeing the protection of the Cathedral and they have, on numerous occasions, prevented serious damage to the building. Most of these incidents were caused by accidental fires (and one infamous deliberate one in 1829 started by the arsonist Jonathan Martin), but even without the fires, the Minster Police have had a tough job over the years ensuring everyone treats the cathedral with respect. A number of peculiar tools were used to ensure citizens obeyed the rules: one police officer called Mr Strutt was known to carry around a flail in order to keep the peace.

In the 1930s the Minster Police stopped being officially sworn in as constables and lost some of their powers of arrest, but these powers have now been reinstated and the officers have the same authority as your regular bobby, just within a smaller precinct.

THE MASON'S LOFT

A doodle studio

York Minster, 8 Minster Yard, YO1 7HL
yorkminster.org
Accessed by private tour, see website for details

Up in the timbers of York Minster is a hidden room, accessed only by private tour, where the master mason once created designs for the magnificent stonework of the Minster. The loft includes a rare tracing floor, original wooden templates and an old medieval toilet that expelled its contents straight out into the Minster Yard.

Every stone carving went through a careful planning process before it was brought to life on the walls of the Minster. The floors were made of soft gypsum and plaster, which meant the mason could trace his ideas directly into the floor and erase any mistakes if needed. It was also easy to add an extra layer of plaster every time the mason wanted a clean surface for more designs. The most recent designs can still be seen in the surface of the floor, as well as imprints from children and pets who may have visited the loft as workers or to keep the workers company.

Constructing cathedral stone was complicated work and needed a strong team of specialised helpers. The master mason would first sketch ideas straight onto the floor of the loft, playing with dimensions and design until he had come up with a clear blueprint. After initial tracing was complete, they would be worked up into wooden templates – many of the originals are still hanging on rails in the mason's loft hundreds of years later. Finally, the designs would be taken to the stonemason's yard to be constructed out of magnesium limestone.

The studio was used until at least the 16th century and acted as both a workshop and an office. It is thought the mason would have invited important people up to the room to present his work and elicit funding or help. The loft was also equipped with all the necessities one might need, including a medieval toilet. This toilet, called a garderobe, was placed in its own narrow corridor to confine the smell as much as possible. Being so high up, an ingenious plumbing system had to be devised. Rainwater was used to flush the contents of the garderobe through a stone pipe that stuck out of the minster walls. It would be emptied down into the yard below. The pipe can still be seen sticking out of the walls.

CHAPTER HOUSE ROOF

Behind the Chapter House ceiling

York Minster, 8 Minster Yard, YO1 7HL
yorkminster.org
Accessed by private tour, see website for details

On walking into the Chapter House of York Minster, it would not be unusual to find a few dedicated tourists lying with their back on the floor taking pictures of its wonderfully photogenic ceiling. Despite the attention the roof gets from below, hardly anyone has seen the other side of it. Yet, the interior of the Chapter House roof is accessible through a secret staircase hidden behind the large Gothic entrance doors (made from English oak 800 years ago, these are the oldest in situ doors in the country) and you can visit it on one of the private tours that the Minster offers.

The top of the stone spiral staircase leads onto the deck of the Minster itself where you can stop to enjoy the views before heading into the Chapter House roof. The pyramid-shaped room is dark and musty – the only natural light comes through small holes in the wall that were designed to admit controlled amounts of oxygen into the space in case of fire. From the platform, there is a 360-degree view of the intricately designed structure: it is a complex mass of timber poles each carved from an oak tree grown around Yorkshire and centred around the central 'king' pole in the middle. It is a brilliant illustration of medieval architecture and engineering; some of the timbers could be 1,000 years old – they would have been fully grown when they were felled to be used for the roof in the 13th century.

The Chapter House was built for use by the York canons, a group of clerics who assisted in the running of the Minster. Each would sit in one of the wall's enclaves: it was built in its octagonal shape to demonstrate that all were considered equal in the decision process. It was also designed to be a splendid, ostentatious structure to demonstrate the ecclesiastical power of York. The roof was originally supposed to be a magnificent stone dome, rather than timber, which is why the supporting wall is over 2 metres thick.

NEARBY
The model of the Chapter House roof
York Minster, 8 Minster Yard, YO1 7HL

At the entrance to the Chapter House is a small model of the roof which lets you appreciate the complete structure without heading into the attic. A human figure is placed where the platform area is: the octagonal maze of wooden pieces that surround him is what you see when you enter the roof. As the sign explains, the king post is surrounded by eight queen posts, eight pendant posts and 16 bosses. The structure was designed on the ground, but then dismantled and rebuilt where it still stands.

OLD PALACE LIBRARY AND ARCHIVE

Largest cathedral library in England

Deans Park, YO1 7JQ
yorkminster.org
By appointment only, see website for details

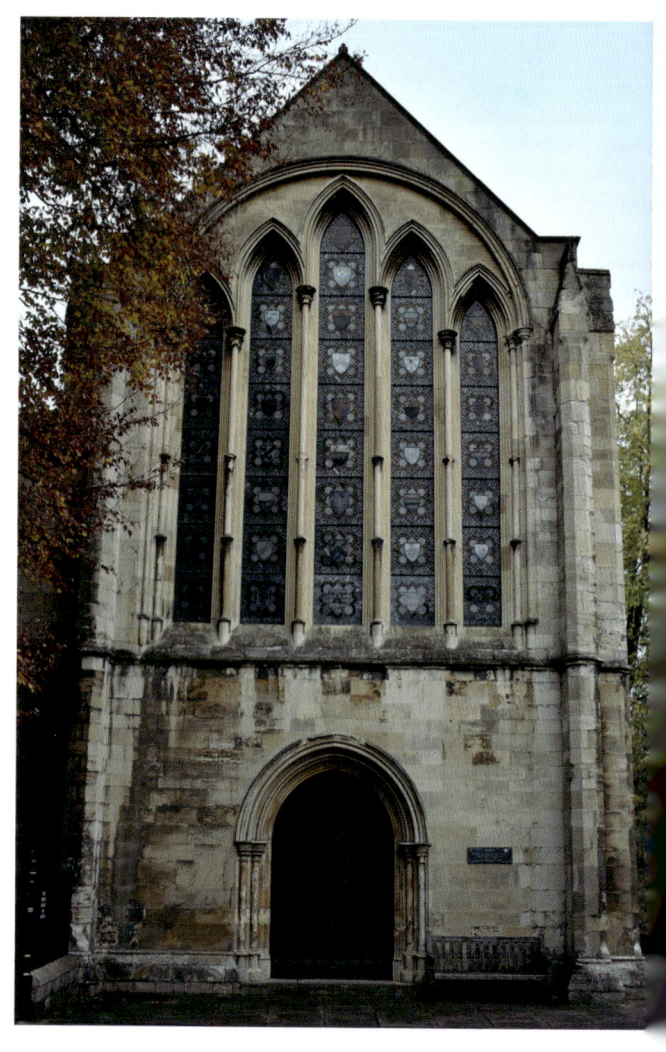

Situated opposite the Minster at the quiet end of Dean's Park is the Old Palace, home to the ancient treasures of York Minster. Its vast archival collections amount to over 130,000 historic books, artefacts, and documents, making it the largest cathedral library in the country. Accessible only by appointment, it is well worth a visit.

The interior of the Old Palace is split into two sections, the historic library and the modern archive. The library has been described as the only one in England that actually smells like a library, probably because it houses a collection of books which has been accumulating for over 600 years. The library and archives are open to anyone interested in viewing historic books, artefacts and documents.

Cathedrals began curating their own personal libraries a few hundred years ago – they were mostly used to lay out the parishes' personal histories, but they also acted as somewhere to hold valuable collections that were not quite suited to public libraries. York's collections were initially housed in the Minster itself but in the 19th century they were moved into their current location. Before being used as a library, this building was originally the chapel of the Archbishop's Palace, hence the name.

One particularly notorious object that remains locked away in the archives is the 'wicked Bible'. Due to a mistake during printing, this copy of the King James Bible encourages infidelity: the sixth commandment orders that 'thou shalt commit adultery'. As punishment for the printing error, the gentleman responsible for printing was fined two years' salary. There are only 12 copies of this adulterous Bible in circulation.

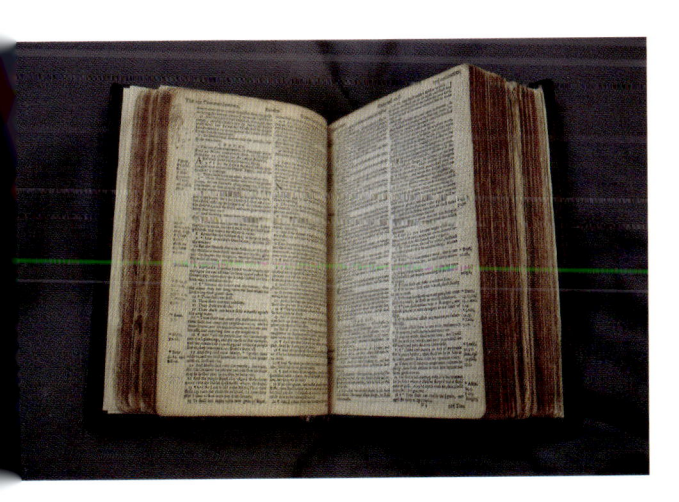

THE HOLY TRINITY CHURCH 24

The candlelit church

Goodramgate, YO1 7LF
visitchurches.org.uk/visit/church-listing/holy-trinity-york.html
Wednesday–Saturday 11am–4pm

Although the Holy Trinity church stands in the middle of a city centre, it is hidden from view behind the shops on Goodramgate. It is a beautiful church, with a neat garden framed by trees and honey-coloured medieval walls, but the interior is even better. Inside, there are plenty of secrets to uncover, including mismatched stained glass, peculiar carvings and the only surviving Georgian pew boxes in the city. Deconsecrated in 1971, there are now only three services held here each year, organised by the Friends of Holy Trinity Goodramgate. The church is frozen in time, and still does not use gas or electricity – candlelight is still the only form of light and heat, which just adds to the romantic nostalgia of the place.

A church was first built on this site in the 12th century, but most of the building you see today dates to more recent reconstructions. During the Victorian restoration of the church, the large stained-glass window that stands behind the altar was split in half and the lower section was moved to the left-hand wall. Unfortunately, the attempt to reassemble the glass in the new wall failed miserably, and many of the pictures became jumbled: you can see that one of the men now has the body of a griffin, and the Virgin Mary has the body of a priest.

The striking dark-wooden pew boxes jut out unevenly along the main aisle. Dating back to the Georgian era, they are the only ones of their kind left in York. The pew-box design was popular as it gave the congregation privacy and protection from drafts; the larger boxes would have been rented by the wealthier families of the parish.

NEARBY

Face of a stonemason

In the first pew box to your right as you enter the church, there is a stone column which takes up a significant amount of space. Although weather-worn, you will be able to make out what looks to be an oddly shaped head carved into the column. It is unknown when the head appeared on the pillar, but he is thought to be the caricatured face of a stonemason, using his finger to wipe dust away from his eye.

BEDERN HALL

Just one 'regular' mistress would be considered acceptable ...

Bartle Garth, St Andrewgate, York YO1 7AL
bedernhall.co.uk
For opening times and admission prices, see website

Bedern Hall is one of those puzzling places that can only be found if you already know where it is, and even once you have been, you will struggle to find again. Accessed either by walking right to the end of Bartle Garth Road (which disguises itself as a cul-de-sac) or through a tiny archway just off Goodramgate, the beautiful medieval hall is now an events space run by the Bedern Hall Company, but was originally built for the Vicars Choral of York Minster in the 13th century as a place of communal dining.

The Vicars Choral was a respected college of men whose role was to sing services at the Minster. Yet, despite their ecclesiastical occupation and the fact that Bedern is an old Anglo-Saxon word for 'house of prayer', the vicars were slightly more liberal than you might expect, even by modern standards. They wore expensive jewels, gambled with dice and were often quite rowdy, usually after having a few pints of ale in the city. On some occasions they were even chased back to Bedern by the city police who, unfortunately for them, did not have jurisdiction over the vicars once they had claimed the sanctuary of the Hall.

The college of vicars were also renowned for their relationships with women. Contact with the fairer sex was officially banned by the leaders of the Church, but this does not seem to have stopped them. The officials had such a hard time getting the college to play by the rules that eventually it was agreed that as long as the men had just one 'regular' mistress, it would be considered acceptable.

After the Reformation it was decided that the vicars would be allowed to marry if they chose to, and many did. The impacts of this can be seen in the architecture of the Hall today. The original arches built into the back wall once led to the pantry which fed the college during their communal dinners, but as individuals married and moved in with families, the number of vicars who dined at Bedern decreased, until the dinner parties were so small that the pantry was no longer needed and the arches were filled in.

THE COFFIN DROP
OF THE GOLDEN SLIPPER PUB

According to medieval superstition, it was bad luck to pass the dead out through the front door of a house

20 Goodramgate, YO1 7LG
Monday–Thursday 12noon–11pm, Friday and Saturday 10am–midnight,
Sunday 10am–11pm

In the front room of the Golden Slipper Pub on Goodramgate, part of the ceiling is slightly lower than that of the rest of the room. As the wooden plaque attached to the lower section of the wall explains, this dip was built in the medieval period as a 'coffin drop', used to assist in lowering coffins from the upstairs room down into the street below.

At the time when the house was built, it was the custom that people who had passed away were laid out to rest in the place that they had died right up until their burial day. According to medieval superstition, it was bad luck to pass the dead out through the front door of a house. Ideally, the coffin would be taken through a side or back door; but the Golden Slipper Pub had a very steep staircase which would have posed a difficult task for the undertakers if people died in one of the upstairs rooms. Ingeniously, a new extension was added to the first storey of the house. This extension hung over the alleyway outside and had detachable floorboards, so that the floor could be opened up and a space could be created for the coffin to pass through. The house became protected from superstition and the removal of the body became slightly more dignified. Although new owners built underneath the coffin drop and the room now part of the interior of the pub, the drop has been preserved for the enjoyment of the diners and the memory of old superstitions.

YORK MINSTER

THE GLASS CASE
OF AN OLD SLIPPER

In order to ward off evil spirits

20 Goodramgate, YO1 7LG
Monday to Thursday 11am–11.30pm, Friday and Saturday 11am–midnight,
Sunday noon–11pm

Underneath the coffin drop of the Golden Slipper Pub is an old slipper lovingly displayed in a glass case alongside a few newspaper clippings. This is the pub's namesake. It dates back to the medieval era and was deliberately placed into the walls of the house in order to ward off evil spirits: according to folklore, a slipper in the wall of a house would also promote happiness and well-being.

NEARBY

The mouse on St William's College

College St, YO1 7JF

If you look closely enough at the doors of St William's College you might see the outline of a wooden mouse clambering up the side. Although St William's looks like an original Tudor building, its timber-fronted walls were rebuilt in the 20th century. The door was created by North Yorkshire's renowned carver, Robert Thompson, also known as the 'Mouseman of Kilburn' because of the animal he chose for a trademark.

THE SIGN OF THE GATEWAY TO THE ROMAN FORTRESS

㉙

Where the Romans came marching in

On the ground of the York walls as you walk anticlockwise from the Monkgate entrance

On the floor of the City Walls, above the junction of Ogleforth Road and Chapter House Street, is a sign which is usually stepped over unnoticed. It marks the point where 5,000 Romans marched into York in 71 AD. When the Ninth Legion of the Roman Army arrived this area was not much more than a large meadow. But, because of its two bordering rivers, the Ouse and the Foss, the Legion saw its strategic potential and chose to base their fortress here. It was the perfect place to defend themselves against the rogue Celtic tribes populating the North of England. Soon enough, they did what the Romans do, and built houses, bathing installations and walls: they called it Eboracum. It was the beginnings of the ancient city we know today, and it all started at this very spot.

THE DUTCH HOUSE

The oldest brick house in York

Ogleforth, YO1 7JG

Formerly known as the 'Small House', this building is now home to the Dutch House Hotel and is thought to be the oldest brick house in York. It was built in the 17th century in the Dutch architectural style, which became popular in England after the ascent of the Dutch Prince William of Orange to the English throne. The building has been used by a number of businesses during its 400 years, but its most important role was the part it played in the history of Yorkshire's famous John Smith's bitter (now part of the Dutch Heineken Group). The building was already being used as a small-scale brewery run by W.H. Thackwray & Co when John Smith Ltd purchased it in 1929. The acquisition formed part of a larger expansion strategy by the beer company to take over local breweries around Yorkshire; the house, along with the two adjoining buildings, became a mini brewery designed to support the larger operation in Tadcaster, a town not far from York. It continued to produce the famous Yorkshire bitter for 11 years until brewing stopped in 1940, most probably due to the impact of World War II on local production: the Old Brewery sign can still be seen next to the house.

The war of the breweries

Yorkshire beer is internationally celebrated, but the personal lives of the Yorkshiremen who started the two leading breweries – John Smith and Samuel Smith – are relatively unknown. John Smith was born in 1824 in North Yorkshire, an entrepreneurial young man who set up a successful brewery in the Tadcaster area. After he died, he left the brewery to his two brothers, William and Samuel. Debates on how they should run the business became heated, and the brothers eventually fell out completely. The bad blood between them was such that William, who had more experience in the industry, decided to build a brand-new brewery right next to the old one, taking all the machinery, workers and even the name John Smith Brewery with him. Samuel Smith stayed on at the old brewery: the two businesses started to compete in a rivalry that continues to this day, with both brewers operating from their original sites in Tadcaster.

THE MERCHANT TAYLORS' HALL ㉛

The Ancient Guild of the Company of Merchant Taylors in the City of York

Aldwark, YO1 7BX
merchant-taylors-york.org
Open on monthly open days or by private appointment, see website for details

Aside from being a beautiful events space, the Merchant Taylors' Hall is a living, if minimalist, museum to one of York's longest-standing ancient guilds. It is only open to the public by private appointment or on the occasional open day, and although there are only a few treasures inside, it is worth a visit to see the original artwork, the replica of the Guild's charter and the old timbers of the 600-year-old hall.

Undoubtedly the star of the show is the large colourful stained-glass window at the front of the Great Hall depicting the Guild's coat of arms. This window was made in 2015 by Helen Whittaker, who also constructed the glass window for Westminster Abbey designed by David Hockney. The Hall's impressive glass display celebrates the 600th anniversary of the Guild. The images on the glass are designed to look as though they have been elaborately stitched together, creating a garment that tells the story of the Taylors – look out for the needle swinging from the final stitch and the silk fabric weaving in and out of the side windows.

Camels might be thought an unusual choice for the coat of arms of a British company, but these animals have been the symbol of the Taylors' Guilds from the start. They were chosen either because the camel is an international symbol of trade, or because of the Taylors' close association with the fraternity of St John the Baptist, who always wore a garment made from camel hair.

The Merchant Taylors were a community of masters and apprentices who started off in the 13th century as three separate guilds: the Taylors, the Drapers and the Hosiers. Each network controlled and influenced their particular trade until the Merchant Taylors' Guild of the City of York was created as an umbrella organisation to bring them all together. The Guild was formalised by King Charles II in the 1662 granting of a Royal Charter; a copy of the original document showing their royal approval hangs at the entrance of the building. The Company of Taylors is now a charity with about 90 members, mostly focused on charitable works, supporting young people in the arts and preserving the ancient hall for future generations.

JEWBURY PLAQUE

Underground cemetery

Foss Bank Carpark, Jewbury, YO31 7PL

> חלקת שדה זו
> היא ב"ית הקברות העתיק של העיר יארק
> מקצת הקברים פונו ולאחר זמן הוזרו ונקברו
> ביום ח' תמוז תשד"ם
> במעמד הרב הכולל וכמה מרבני המדינה
>
> THIS IS THE LOCATION OF THE ANCIENT
> JEWISH CEMETERY OF YORK
> SOME OF THE REMAINS WERE RE-INTERRED
> 8TH JULY 1984 — 8TH TAMMUZ 5744
> IN THE PRESENCE OF THE CHIEF RABBI
> SIR IMMANUEL JAKOBOVITS
> AND REPRESENTATIVES OF
> THE JEWISH COMMUNITY.
> THE RE-INTERMENT SITE WAS KINDLY
> PROVIDED BY J SAINSBURY PLC,
> TO WHOM THE JEWISH COMMUNITY
> IS MOST GRATEFUL
>
> ב"ה הקברות נמשך להלן תהת העמודי"ם
>
> THE ANCIENT CEMETERY APPROXIMATED
> TO THE PRESENT CAR PARK AREA

The mass of shoppers heading into Sainsbury's multi-storey carpark tend to drive past the Jewbury memorial plaque without a second glance. This large granite tribute hanging on the wall next to the entranceway marks a medieval Jewish cemetery which still lies below the concrete floor where locals buy their weekly groceries.

Medieval Jewish cemeteries in the North of England were unusual because until the 12th century the bodies of the recently deceased had to be sent all the way down to the central cemetery in London. It was only when King Henry II granted the Jewish community the right to a private burial place within every city that they began to arrange for loved ones to be buried in ground nearer their homes. It was an important step for a group that had long been marginalised, and the York community were quick to organise a secluded cemetery within an area called Jewbury, literally meaning the Jewish quarter.

Except for a few surviving documents that hinted at a possible burial ground, no one could be sure that the ancient cemetery actually existed. It was only when the supermarket chain submitted its plans to develop the site in the 1980s, and the York Archaeological Trust was asked to complete an exploration of the area, that the remains of a mass burial ground – estimated to be the burial place of around 1,000 people – was discovered.

It was initially debated at the higher levels of the Jewish community whether or not the cemetery was indeed Jewish, as the graves were not conventionally Jewish: they did not face Jerusalem and the coffins had iron nails instead of the wooden pegs that experts would have expected to see. However, the excavated remains were found in simple graves in accordance with the Jewish tradition, and there was enough evidence to convince the Chief Rabbi of England, Immanuel Jakobovits, of its true origins. After it was confirmed as a Jewish cemetery, the excavations were stopped in order to allow the souls to rest in peace in the place where they were buried. The cemetery is the only one of its kind to have been excavated by archaeologists, which makes it of national importance in terms of understanding a little-known historic community.

ST ANTHONY'S GARDEN

A secret garden

St Anthony's Hall
Peasholme Green, YO1 7PW

Below the City Walls, the garden of St Anthony's Hall is a secret garden designed for the senses. Full to bursting with aromatic herbs, textured plants and bright colours, the garden won the York Design Award in 2009, although it is still generally unknown and thus often completely empty. Sitting alongside a naturalised meadow, woodland trees, a water rill, sculptures and a summerhouse, St Anthony's garden is one of the most calming places in the city.

The garden is owned by the York Conservation Trust, and is situated in the grounds of St Anthony's Hall, a former guildhall, prison, workhouse, school and now exhibition space. The garden itself was once the concrete playground of St Anthony's School, but when the Trust bought the grounds in 2006, they decided to create a sensory space for the public. They planted sweet smelling lavender and thyme next to the soft foliage of lamb's ear in order to create an experience of nature which anyone, especially the visually imparied, could enjoy. As well as the scented and tactile plants, a few symbolic designs are incorporated into the garden. The stone wall represents the path of life, starting with the security of the low enclosure, then leading you up and down until you reach the highest point of the Tau Cross which symbolically heals you after your long journey.

Kings Square – Castle

①	ARUP BUILDING	76
②	NORTH EASTERN RAILWAY WAR MEMORIAL	78
③	GEORGE LEEMAN STATUE	80
④	THE DOORS OF THE YORK GRAND HOTEL BASEMENT	81
⑤	CHOLERA BURIAL GROUND	82
⑥	JOHN SNOW'S PUMP	83
⑦	SNEAK HOLES OF ALL SAINTS CHURCH	84
⑧	JACOB'S WELL	86
⑨	BISHOPHILL COMMUNITY GARDEN	88
⑩	LADY ANNE'S EFFIGY	90
⑪	CAT SCULPTURES	92
⑫	YORK DRILL AND ARMY MUSEUM	94
⑬	PRISONERS' SIGNATURES	96

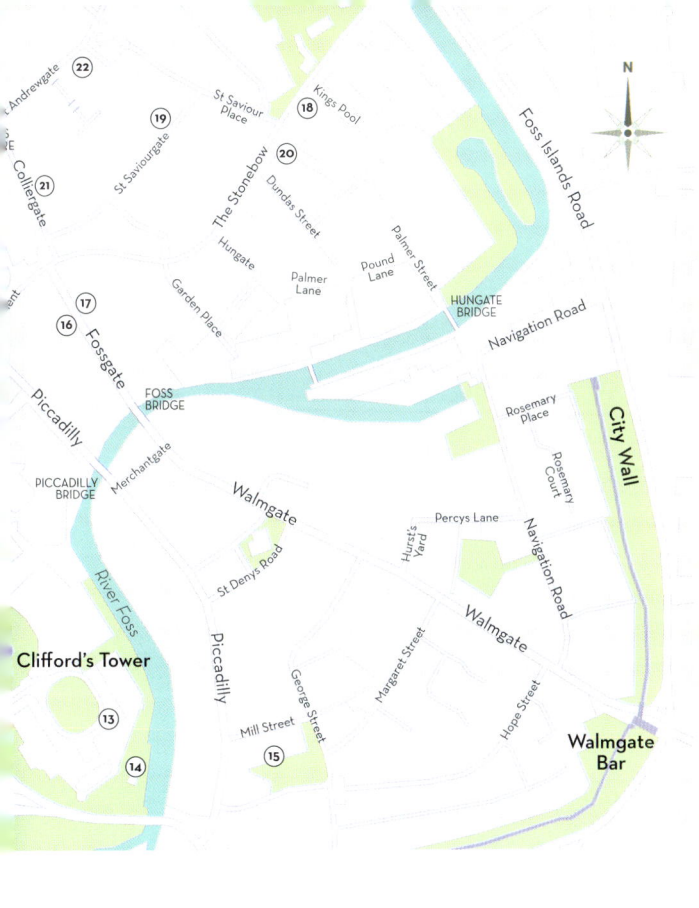

⑭	RAINDALE MILL	98
⑮	DICK TURPIN'S FAKE GRAVE	100
⑯	LADY PECKETT'S YARD	102
⑰	MORRELL YARD	104
⑱	CLAY PIPE AT THE BLACK SWAN INN	106
⑲	UNITARIAN CHAPEL	108
⑳	THE ROCKET IN THE HISCOX BUILDING	110
㉑	INSCRIPTION OF THE ANCIENT SOCIETY OF FLORISTS	111
㉒	ST ANDREW'S DRILL HALL	112
㉓	ROMAN BATH MUSEUM	114
㉔	SIGNED BRICKS	116
㉕	THE COUNCIL CHAMBER	118
㉖	COLUMN OF THE GEORGE INN	120
㉗	BETTYS' MIRROR	122
㉘	THE MANSION HOUSE CAT	124

ARUP BUILDING

①

Former stable building

Lendal Arches
Tanner's Moat, YO1 6HU

The front view of the Arup office is striking. But the original purpose of the building is even more unusual. This 19th-century building was once home to Botterill's Horse and Carriage Repository, York's multi-storey carpark for horses.

In the early 20th century, when automobiles were new, slow and unreliable, a horse-and-carriage was still the go-to travel plan. Gentlemen would journey into York on their steeds and needed somewhere to leave them as they went about their business. This is where Botterill's came in. While their owners were busy, the horses would be led in through the arches, taken up to one of the several upper floors on a spiral ramp and checked into one of Botterill's 200 stalls. Passers-by would be able to see their friendly equine faces peeking out from between the arches.

Tourists would also use Botterill's to rent a horse-and-carriage while they were in the city, and the building often hosted well-attended horse auctions. With the decline in horse travel, Botterill's closed and the building ended up being partly demolished in 1965 in order to be used as a car dealership, leaving only two arches remaining.

The design of the building was considered rather bold at the time. Originally, there were more storeys on top of the building and the architect, W.G. Pentry, was extravagant with the embellishments. The building was designed in a distinct Byzantine style, with Gothic brickwork, elaborate bright colours and decorative ornate features – rather a change from York's previous cityscape.

Reproduced from an original held by City of York Council / Explore Libraries and Archives Mutual, York.

NORTH EASTERN RAILWAY WAR MEMORIAL

The competition of remembrance

Station Road, YO1 6FZ

On the south side of the river, two First World War memorials are in very close proximity: the one on Station Road and the one in Memorial Gardens.

The two tributes were initially both going to be built on Station Road, but due to the difference in scale, the city council thought it prudent to move their memorial to a place where it would not be so obviously compared. Although ending in compromise, the design and building process saw a fair number of heated debates between the company and the council about the imbalance between the two.

It was fairly common for business organisations to have their own war memorials to honour the employees who fought and died in battle, and North Eastern Railway (NER) – which operated from York – had the fourth largest railway workforce in the country. They lost many employees during the war and understandably wanted to build a monument to commemorate them. The location was decided upon: it was to be built at the top of Station Road on land belonging to the NER, just up the street from where the City Council planned to place their memorial.

As with most things, the disparity between the two memorials all came down to funds. Being such a large private enterprise, NER had more money to hand than the cash-strapped city council. The famous architect Sir Edwin Lutyens (who designed 58 war memorials around the country) was commissioned to lead the project. Lutyens enthusiastically began the task and created a colossal design based on a secular altar, including a Great War Stone and a screen for the soldiers' names. Lutyens was also appointed to design the city war memorial, but given the smaller budget, they had to make do with a simple obelisk and cross. After comparing the two memorials, supporters of the city attempted to find some objection to NER's and have it moved, but they did not get very far. To smooth things over, NER donated some of their land as a location for the city's memorial so the two would not be comparable, and the city's obelisk found a home in Memorial Gardens.

GEORGE LEEMAN STATUE

A 'hopeless imbecile' or a dodgy businessman?

Station Rise, YO1 6GD

The rivalry between George Leeman and George Hudson was legendary in political circles. One was a Liberal, the other a Tory. Both served as mayor of York. Both were key individuals in York's railway history. Only one ended up with a statue.

There has long been a conspiracy theory that the George Leeman statue which stands on Station Rise is actually his political and business rival, George Hudson. Rumour has it that the statue was created in Hudson's honour after he died, but because he had become a social outcast following the discovery of some dubious business deals (after an investigation led by Leeman), the statue was hidden away. After Leeman's death, the effigy was apparently altered to look more like Leeman and brought out with the hope that no one would notice the difference.

As fun as this would be, the rumours are sadly not true. For one thing, the statue would have had to have grown hair and lost weight. For another, there is evidence which details the creation of the statue in Leeman's image, and it went through a very rigorous process to make absolutely sure that it looked like the man himself. The artist, George Milburn, had to create a model of his sculpture before it was approved by the memorial committee. Although they agreed to his design, public criticism said that the model was not a very flattering portrait of the man – one observer said it looked like 'a hopeless imbecile'. Milburn was told he had to improve the likeness, or he would not only be replaced as the artist but would also have to fund the replacement statue. Luckily for Milburn, his techniques improved dramatically, the model became a good likeness and the statue was approved.

NEARBY

The doors of the York Grand Hotel basement (4)

Station Rise, YO1 6GD

Beneath the floors of York's only five-star hotel are old vaults that once held millions of pounds in lucrative railway profits. Now part of a luxury spa, the heavy doors of the manicure room are reminders of York's Edwardian days, when they held the treasures of the North Eastern Railway company (NER). The Grand (which opened in 2010) was originally the NER headquarters, and the old HQ-turned-hotel is a fantastic place to explore: you can usually pop down to the basement to see the vaults without booking a spa treatment, as long as it is not too busy.

CHOLERA BURIAL GROUND

⑤

The city's grave

Station Rise, YO1 6GD

Next to a busy road on the way to the railway station, the Cholera Burial Ground is mostly ignored by the commuters rushing to get their train. If they were to stop, they would see a grim reminder of the 19th-century global cholera epidemic.

Every one of the people buried in the graveyard was a victim of York's first cholera epidemic. Normally, you would expect to find these lost souls in churchyards, but the burial ground has survived in this odd location because of an agreement made between the church and the City of York almost 200 years ago.

Thought to have started in South Asia around 1826, cholera took over five years to cross Europe and spread to England. Because travel (even for disease) was so much slower back then, York had time to prepare as best it could. Lectures were given, the Board of Health was started and inspectors were hired to check on conditions. Unfortunately, no one really knew anything about the disease, so despite these precautions the epidemic soon hit hard. With church graveyards reaching capacity and bodies piling up, the local government had to step in to ensure that there was enough burial space for the increasing number of victims.

A spot of land was chosen for the new graves, but because the authority of all burials had to fall under the jurisdiction of the church, the land was technically being rented to the archbishop from the government – the question now was how long the lease should last. Some members of the council wanted the land spiritually protected by the archbishop for 60 years and then given back to the city. Others argued that it must remain sacred land forever. Eventually it was agreed that the graves would never be moved, no matter what changes were made around them, which is why there is now a small graveyard between a busy main road and the City Walls.

NEARBY
John Snow's pump (6)
North Street, YO1 6JD

Close to the house where he grew up is a memorial to the man who identified the cause of cholera. John Snow was born into poverty as the son of a coal miner but became a successful doctor and set up his own practice in London. Snow believed that cholera was waterborne and he convinced the London Broad Street Council to remove the handle on the local Broad Street pump so that people would not have access to unclean water. The infection rate went down, knowledge about the disease went up and eventually a cure was found. Snow was the man who 'took the handle off the Broad Street Pump' and saved thousands of lives. The memorial in York is a replica of the Broad Street pump. For more information about the London cholera pump, see *Secret London, an unusual guide* from the same publisher.

SNEAK HOLES OF ALL SAINTS CHURCH

A window to the inside

North Street, YO1 6JD
Access possible by request if the church is not too busy
allsaints-northstreet.org.uk

At the very back of the 11th-century All Saints North Street Church are a few fascinating windows which are significantly less famous than their colourful stained-glass counterparts. A tiny square window can be found high up on the wall to the left of the entrance. Known as a 'sneak hole' or 'squint', it once acted as a viewing point into the nave from a private dwelling which adjoined the church, and gave the occupant a clear view of the altar and of the celebration of mass. This dwelling has recently been reconstructed and by request you can go around the back to see it from the outside or up to the room itself to peer through the squint into the church.

The original dwelling and squint were built in the 15th century for Dame Emma Raughton. Dame Emma was a deeply religious woman who lived as a hermit, refusing all contact with the outside world and remaining inside her room at all times. This extreme isolation allowed her to focus all her energy on prayer and contemplation. She had several religious 'visions' throughout her life and acted as spiritual adviser to a number of important political figures, including the Earl of Warwick, who was one of the most powerful men in England.

This sacrificial role was officially referred to as an 'Anchoress' (which comes from the Greek word *anachoretes* meaning 'one who lives apart'). They were not unusual in the medieval period: as many as seven 'anchorholds' were occupied in York during this time and they were seen as important pillars of the community. The Archbishop of York himself presided over the ceremony to 'brick up' Anchoress Dame Emma inside the walls of her house, dependent for the rest of her life on donations of food and clothes and the squint for interaction with the outside world.

NEARBY

The half-smoked angel of All Saints Church

In 1997 All Saints Church disastrously caught fire. The blaze quickly consumed half the church, and it was thought that the entire structure would collapse. However, once the flames reached the first angel on the ceiling canopy, the fire stopped and did not go further – although the angel is half-smoked, he is still standing, having successfully stopped the fire in its tracks.

JACOB'S WELL

(8)

The house worth a single rose

5 Trinity Lane, YO1 6EL
jacobswellyork.org
Every other Wednesday 10am–12.30pm or by private appointment

Tucked away next to the gardens of the Holy Trinity Church is the timber-framed lodge called Jacob's Well. The combination of its location on the quiet residential road of Trinity Lane and the long list of better-known medieval attractions in the area has meant that this modest little house is often overlooked, yet Jacob's Well has been officially recognised as one of the most important properties in the city due to its intriguing history and unique architectural features.

The house was originally built as a place of private worship for the Benedictine Monks of Holy Trinity Priory: to the right of the house, you will see a private entrance leading to Holy Trinity Church.

In the 16th century, the Priory itself was disbanded by King Henry VIII as part of the dissolution of the monasteries and the house was put up for sale.

It was purchased by Dame Isabella Ward, the wealthy prioress of York's Clementhorpe Nunnery who, after retiring from monastic life, gifted the land to her charity trustees. Isabella continued to lodge in the house until she passed away three years later, paying a peppercorn rent each year on Midsummer's Day in the form of a single red rose.

The charm of the building continued even after it was converted to an alehouse in the 1800s, during which time it was given the name Jacob's Well, as seen on the simple black sign outside the entrance. It is thought that this name was chosen to promote the inn as a place of romantic chance encounters through the connection to the biblical story of Jacob and Rachel who fell in love by the side of a well while Rachel was watering her father's sheep.

The Micklegate parish took on ownership of Jacob's Well when the inn lost its licence in 1904, re-establishing the link to the Holy Trinity Church, which remains to this day.

Comic carvings

The unique 15th-century wooden canopy that hangs over the entrance to Jacob's Well was added in the 1900s. It is not known who designed it, but they certainly had an odd sense of humour, as among the more traditional carvings – an angel, an eagle, a rose – you will see on the right-hand corner of the canopy a moulding of a heated argument between a husband and wife. On the opposite side, the husband has been replaced with what looks like a coffin next to what appears to be a very happy widow!

Carvings of quarrelsome and even violent interactions between the sexes were common in medieval architecture and can be seen in other examples throughout the city, most notably on the sculptures around York Minster.

BISHOPHILL COMMUNITY GARDEN

A secret hideaway that used to be a churchyard

Bishophill Senior Road, YO1 6HN

The atmosphere of Bishophill Community Garden can be spooky – it functions like a public park, with benches and open spaces, and yet it is dotted with graves and surrounded by black iron gates that are accessed from the main road by a narrow snickleway (a York alleyway). The garden is on a rather quiet street, in a particularly quiet corner of York, but the unusual atmosphere of this secret hideaway is mostly due to the fact that Bishophill Community Garden used to be a churchyard, and yet the church is nowhere to be seen.

The old church, St Mary Bishophill Senior, was built before the Norman conquest, but it became progressively destroyed by severe thunderstorms, neglect, and a declining parish. It was demolished in the 1960s after a long debate around its historical importance, leaving a peaceful and unusual community space for local activities. Stone slabs are still set into the grass, outlining the blueprint of what was St Mary Bishophill Senior Church. There are also said to be Roman remains under the lawn, potentially from a Roman church. Some people even believe that it was the location of York's very first minster. The garden is now owned by York City Council and protected as an archaeological site. Nevertheless, as long as the amateur horticulturalists do not dig too deep, the community garden group can use the churchyard as they like: it is mostly used for minor planting projects and quiet contemplation. The community has shaped out three main areas for the different uses of the space – a patch for planting, a lawn for recreation, and an area of protected wilderness.

> Running down alongside the gates of Bishopshill Community Garden is a prime example of a York snickelway. Snickelways are small medieval passages that run all around the city, connecting the streets and roads together in a maze of concealed paths. They were first explained by local author Mark Jones in 1983 as 'narrow places to walk along, leading from somewhere to somewhere else' but the actual definition of a 'snickelway' is hard to pin down. The expression itself comes from a blending of the words 'snicket', 'ginnel' and 'alleyway'.

LADY ANNE'S EFFIGY

Hospital for widows

Middletons Hotel, Cromwell Road, YO1 6DS

As you walk up the path to the entrance of Middletons Hotel, a white statue of a woman in a rather unusual hat will be looking down on you. This is Dame Anne Middleton, the hotel's namesake, who set up the Middleton hospital on this site in the 17th century: her effigy has watched over the place ever since.

Married to the Sheriff of York, Dame Anne's status and wealth are clearly shown by the choice of clothes that she is wearing in her effigy. The semi-masculine broad-brimmed hat, doublet and ruff around her neck were typical of the 17th century, displaying some of the more impractical fashion trends exclusively available to the rich. Lady Middleton outlived her husband, and after the Sheriff passed away she used part of the money left to her to build a private hospital (almshouse) exclusively for the widows of the Freemasons of York.

A free national healthcare service was still a few hundred years away when the hospital was built and almshouses set up by wealthy individuals were fairly common, ensuring that people from all walks of life were looked after in sickness and old age. The hospital experienced a few changes in the 1800s which saw most of the original building knocked down. By 1972 the place was almost derelict. It was sold to new buyers who sympathetically refurbished the buildings and created the hotel complex you see today, which includes six historically protected buildings in the small area around the old hospital. The whole site is said to form the largest building in York after the Minster.

NEARBY

Chaplin House staircase

Middletons Hotel, Cromwell Road, YO1 6DS

Next to Lady Anne's effigy, Chaplin House is also part of the Middletons Hotel complex. Formerly the home of the director of York City Art Gallery, an art expert called Hans Hess, it was renamed Chaplin House when it was acquired by the hotel, supposedly because Charlie Chaplin himself once stayed there. The white staircase leading up its three floors is noted as the architectural highlight of the hotel, as it dates back to the 17th century. To the untrained eye it is difficult to appreciate the beauty of the 'swept handrail', 'detailed balusters' (the vertical rods in between floor and rail) and the 'square knops' (the corner bits at the top), but it would probably delight the staircase critics of the world.

CAT SCULPTURES

The York Cat Trail

Low Ousegate 9–11, YO1 9QX
Cat trail maps available at The Cat Gallery, 45 Low Petergate
Monday–Friday 10am–5pm

Playfully scampering over various buildings around the city are 2 cats that are said to bring luck to those who find them.

All unique with their own identities and stories behind them, the two cats climbing the walls of Low Ousegate were the first to appear in the city. They were made in the early 1900s for Sir Stephen Aitcheson as decorative ornaments to brighten up the walls of the buildings he owned, with the added benefit of scaring away pigeons from the windowsills.

A local architect called Tom Adams was the leading force behind the York cats from the 1970s onwards. Adams had been using the black cat as a signature for 20 years before he hired sculptor Jonathan Newdick to create life-sized statues to put on his buildings. It is said that Newdick based his designs on cats that he visited at the York RSPCA animal home, and each sculpture displays the feline personality of its original.

Interest in decorative cat sculptures grew after Adams's statues became a familiar sight in the city, and many other individuals began placing similar moggies on their own houses and businesses. Some are wooden carvings rather than metal statues, a few have companions alongside them, and one is even used as a door handle.

Several of the cats have disappeared over the years, but most have made their way back to their homes safe and sound, usually without any explanation for their mysterious adventures. The original black cat you can see on Low Ousegate was stolen in 1984 by an opportunistic thief who climbed onto the temporary scaffolding attached to the shop next door in order to reach it. In the morning, all that remained on the wall was a little white paw. Luckily, it was found a few days later by a local teacher and returned to its rightful place.

Half a cat

The only kitten in the clowder of cats can be found on the house at ½ St Andrew Gate, just off King's Square. Designed as a mini sculpture due to its unusual address, this is one of Tom Adams and Jonathan Newdick's creations.

The York Cat Trail map

All the current 23 felines that can be found in the city have now been connected by the York Cat Trail, a useful map describing each of the cats and their locations. Started in 2010 by Keith Mulhearn, owner of the tour company Complete Yorkshire, the most recent edition of the York Cat Trail can be picked up at The Cat Gallery on Low Petergate.

YORK DRILL AND ARMY MUSEUM

Battles and flags

3 Tower Street, YO1 9SB
yorkarmymuseum.co.uk
See website for opening times and admission fees

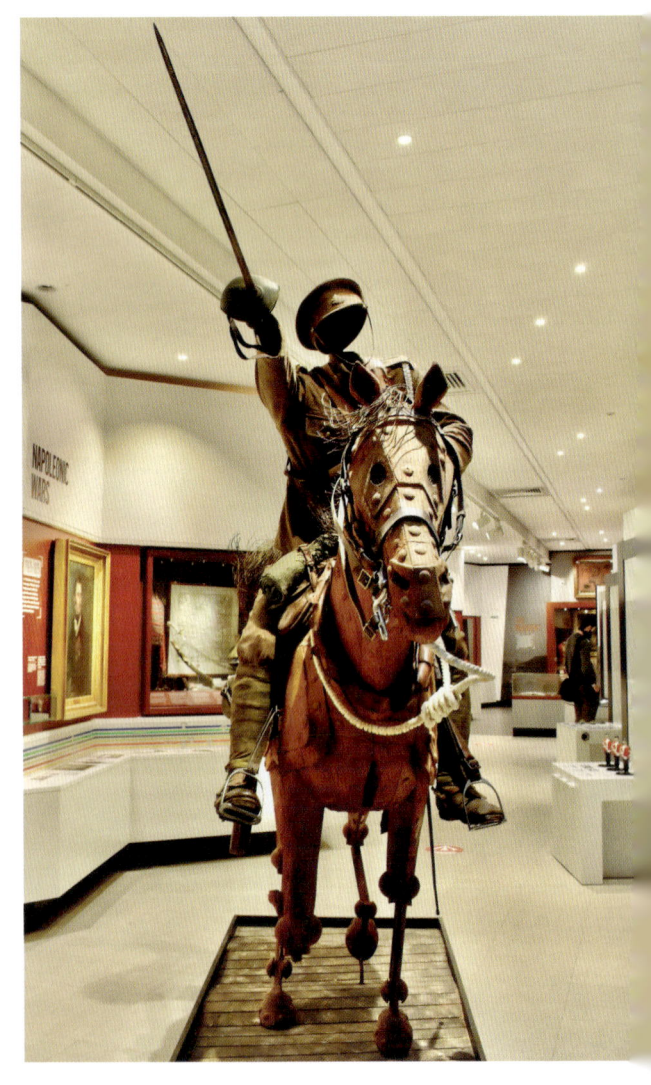

Squeezed between a hotel and the York Regimental Headquarters, the York Drill and Army Museum is situated in the basement of what looks like a domestic home. The museum traces the history of two of Yorkshire's military regiments and its specialised nature means it is often unfairly overlooked when compared to the famous Castle Museum across the road. The building itself, called The Drill Hall, was purposely built as the headquarters for the 1st East Riding of Yorkshire Artillery Volunteers in 1885 and subsequently acted as HQ for the Yorkshire Regiments. A museum was added in the 1980s, and having gone through a recent refurbishment (courtesy of the Heritage Lottery Fund), it is now impressively decked out with display cabinets and interactive exhibits.

The Prince of Wales's Own Yorkshire Regiment and The Royal Dragoon Guards are parts of the British Army which can trace their ancestry back to a regiment set up by King James II. Beginning in the 17th century, when the Dragoons were so named because the smoke that came out of their muskets reminded the men of dragons, the museum tells the story of the regiments' 300-year evolution, following their military lives through letters, battles, uniforms, medals and weapons. It gives the visitor a wider understanding of the individual experience of war as well as the usual battle dates and figures.

The pride of the museum is an antique flag called the Dettingen Standard which lies protected under a thick glass case. Given the symbolic importance of the standard in battle, the 'bearer' of the flag would always end up being one of the key targets for the opposing forces – forming a life-or-death version of the game 'capture the flag' whereby each regiment would aim to retrieve the standard of the opposing side. This particular standard was used in the Battle of Dettingen in 1743 – it was the last battle which saw a British King, George II, personally lead his forces into war, and is the oldest cavalry standard in existence.

PRISONERS' SIGNATURES

The convicts' graffiti

Castle Museum
Tower Street, YO1 8RY
yorkcastlemuseum.org.uk
For opening times see website for details

Scratched into the walls and floors of the family-friendly Castle Museum are the names and initials of York's historic criminals. Although somewhat hidden from view, you can still see them particularly well in the paving of the courtyard or behind the displays of the psychedelic 1960s memorabilia room. Long ago, the Castle Museum once had another life as a prison. It was built in the 18th century and usually held inmates awaiting trial, most of whom were locked up for failing to pay their debts. Women and men were both held here, but in separate sections of the building.

The museum has embraced its historic identity through an interactive exhibition in its basement which tells the individual stories of particular convicts through holographs. One of the stories you can hear is that of Simon Hargreaves, whose signature can be found on the wall just before the entrance of the basement. Hargreaves was what we nowadays might call a 'lager lout'. He was sent to the prison for breaking into a house and stealing someone's breakfast – he was actually arrested with a boiled egg in his pocket. During his time at the prison, he remained rebellious – note the graffiti – and was unfortunately found guilty and transported to Tasmania as a convict. Luckily for him, once he had finished his jail time, he married, started a family and created a successful coach-building business. Sadly, not all the prisoners whose signatures you see on the wall lived happily ever after: many of these stories ended abruptly on the gallows, leaving the signatures as the only lasting memorial they have.

NEARBY

Taxidermy of an English Shepherd

Castle Museum, Tower Street, YO1 8RY

The first display you see on your way around the museum is an example of a rural Victorian home. Every single object in the exhibit comes from the Victorian period, except one. The English Shepherd lying contentedly by the fire appeared in 1960, after he was donated to the museum by his owner. When Guinness the dog was alive, he was a regular at the museum and used to visit on a weekly basis alongside his owner. But when he passed away, the family could not stand the thought of burying him, so Guinness was stuffed and donated to the museum where he could be visited by people every day.

RAINDALE MILL

The travelling water mill

Accessed through Castle Museum
Tower Street, YO1 8RY
yorkcastlemuseum.org.uk
Can be seen from Tower Street Bridge, YO1 9RY
Check website for opening times

On the grassy bank between the Castle Museum and the River Foss, few people know of the existence of a tiny building called Raindale Mill, let alone the story of its long journey to get there. The mill started off life in Raindale Valley, a secluded area of the North Yorkshire Moors, where it was built as a cottage-cum-mill with the simple purpose of meeting local demands for flour and animal feed. Production stopped after the river that generated the mill's power changed course, and it stood empty for 20 years until the whole structure was offered to the York Castle Museum in 1935 as an example of small-scale Victorian manufacturing.

At this time, John Kirk, the museum owner, was obsessively

collecting historic pieces as part of his ambition to create a real-life Victorian town – which now forms Kirk Street, the main attraction in the museum – so he was very keen to have the mill transferred over. His project was interrupted by World War II – the relocation of the mill did not take place until the 1950s.

Getting the little mill to York involved a painfully slow manual process, which took over a week, with five men setting off each day on a forty-mile drive to get to the secluded Raindale Valley and then having a mile-long hike along a railway track to reach the spot where it stood. The mill was completely neglected and had started rotting away, but they dismantled the bricks and brought the machinery back to begin the arduous task of rebuilding it to its former glory. The mill was opened to the public in the mid-1960s but closed relatively quickly after health and safety concerns mounted. The 2000s saw a significant reconstruction project that not only got the mill working again, but improved the gardens around the cottage. The mill was re-opened, and now volunteers well-versed in the art of Victorian milling teach the public how to grind flour the old-fashioned way.

DICK TURPIN'S FAKE GRAVE

⑮

A fake grave functioning as a focal point for tourist pilgrimage

St George's Churchyard, 6 Lead Mill Lane, YO1 9QH

Dick Turpin (1705–1739) has been remembered in popular culture as something of a Robin Hood-type figure: a dashing highwayman who stole from the rich and gave to the poor, 'careless to results, indifferent to obstacles, ever on the alert'.

The popular story of the Essex-born butcher's son who fell into a life of crime and grew into the infamous Yorkshire robber has put Dick Turpin's grave in the grounds of St George's Churchyard high on the tourist bucket list of the city. However, the headstone marking Turpin's burial spot might actually be as mythical as his glamourised life. Dick Turpin, who went under the pseudonym of John Palmer, was hanged on York's Knavesmire fields in 1739 for the crime of stealing a horse (quite a light offence compared to the years of robbery and murder); his body was taken to St George's graveyard to be buried.

His death seems to have been quite the event, with huge crowds gathered to watch the legendary highwayman be led to the gallows – Turpin even paid a few extra mourners to attend his execution and add some emotion to the scene. Some days after the funeral, Turpin's body became the victim of the widespread crime of grave-robbing, which saw unscrupulous doctors pay large amounts of cash for recently deceased bodies in order to dissect them in the name of scientific research. The culprits (or 'resurrection men') were soon discovered and Turpin's body had to be re-buried.

Even with the effects of the double-burial, the area that now marks Dick Turpin's grave seems unusually large in contrast with the others in the graveyard. Rumour has it that the grave was made so large so that he could be buried with his beloved horse, Black Bess. But Bess was also part of the Dick Turpin myth, created and popularised in the 1800s by the author William Harrison Ainsworth, so it is unlikely that there is a horse down there. Additionally, experts believe that the headstone is newer than the other graves surrounding it and was probably made almost 200 years after Turpin's death. It is now thought that the grave was put there as a focal point for tourist pilgrimages, and the body is actually buried in some other unmarked spot in the churchyard, safe from tourists and grave-robbers alike.

RICHARD TURPIN *Shooting a Man near his Cave on Epping Forest.*

LADY PECKETT'S YARD

The forgotten alley

Pavement, YO1 9UP

Taken straight out of a scene from *Harry Potter*, for some reason the snickleway (a York alleyway) called Lady Peckett's Yard is not nearly so well known as the famous Shambles. It has the same medieval atmosphere, with none of the tourist traffic, and it almost feels as though you are trespassing on a private courtyard.

The passage was once two alleys, one running from Pavement and one from Fossgate. One was originally called *Bacusgail* (or Bake House Lane) after the businesses that were run here, and the other was *Trichourgail* (or Cheat's Lane) from the Old English word for 'traitor', which probably refers to some unknown event now lost in time.

The name was changed to Lady Peckett's Yard in the late 18th century, after the wife of a previous Lord Mayor of York who lived in one of the houses after he had died. There is not much information about Lady Alice Peckett herself, although she apparently still haunts the Golden Fleece pub next door. The alley buildings are mostly occupied by commercial businesses, but No. 11 is now owned by the York Conservation Trust. This was the location where Joseph Rowntree (of Rowntree's Chocolate), set up York's first charitable school for adults, teaching the lower classes to read and write.

A local legend has been passed down the generations (without much evidence to back it up) which tells the tale of a fully grown lion escaping from a nearby circus and finding its way to Lady Peckett's Yard. Being so narrow, the alleyway gave the police an opportunity to trap the big cat, and it was eventually given back to its owners.

MORRELL YARD

A quiet courtyard off a busy street

Morrell Yard, Fossgate, YO1 9TW

Fossgate is York's social hub. Open almost any door on the street and it will lead you into a trendy café, cocktail bar, historic pub, fancy restaurant or an eclectic independent shop. There is one entrance, however, that takes you somewhere entirely different. Behind the green door signposted Morrell Yard is a quiet enclosure dedicated to the founders of the York Conservation Trust, the celebrated charity set up to protect York's historic buildings.

Filled with flowers and potted plants, this small commemorative courtyard provides a brief respite from the energetic atmosphere outside. Composed of ten dwellings, a courtyard and a medieval stone well, this space has been owned by the York Conservation Trust since 1996. It was dedicated to the founders of the Trust, John and Cuthbert Morrell. A black sign attached to the wall of the courtyard gives a brief overview of when the trust was founded and when the yard was opened.

The York Conservation Trust

In 1945 brothers John and Cuthbert Morrell created a company that bought and restored seven old medieval buildings around York. After they died, responsibility for the company was passed down through the Morrell family. In 1976 the company became a charity under the name the York Conservation Trust: it now owns over 85 buildings, all identifiable by the Trust's forest-green emblem which will be placed somewhere on the outside.

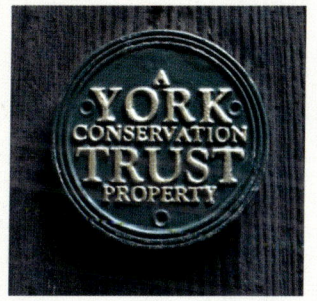

CLAY PIPE
AT THE BLACK SWAN INN

The smoking ghost

23 Peasholme Green, YO1 7PR
blackswanyork.com
Monday–Saturday noon–11pm, Sunday noon–10.30pm

Being one of the oldest pubs in York, the Black Swan Inn has unsurprisingly accumulated countless curiosities and secrets since it was first built in 1417. In true York tradition, the most interesting stories that you hear about the medieval inn relate to its long and colourful history with ghosts – in particular, the tale of the old clay pipe that can be found protected by a glass case in the cosy back room of the pub.

The pipe hangs next to the large 17th-century fireplace and blends in with the assorted pictures that decorate the room. It was discovered under the floorboards of the pub during a renovation project in 2003 by the builders who were working on the site. The workers, thinking nothing of the artefact, went to throw it away. Yet as they did so, an icy chill fell on the room. The atmosphere did not return to normal until the pipe was restored to the place where it was discovered. It remains protected in that very spot to this day, often unnoticed by the diners and drinkers.

It is still not known how the pipe came to be there, but it might well be linked to the other interesting stories that feature in the pub's long history. Maybe it was owned by a spectator at the weekly illegal cockfights that once took place in the attic room; perhaps it was dropped by one of the more liberal members of the congregation of St Cuthbert's Church as they crept through the underground passageway that is thought to have connected the church and the pub; or it could have just belonged to one of the regulars who, even when he passed away, did not want to leave his favourite watering hole.

A local folk singer at the pub was inspired to write the story of the unknown owner, and the poem now sits under the pipe, fuelling the unanswered mystery of the Smoking Ghost.

UNITARIAN CHAPEL

⑲

The oldest surviving non-conformist church in York

31 St Saviourgate, YO1 8NQ
yorkunitarians.org.uk
For opening times and events see website

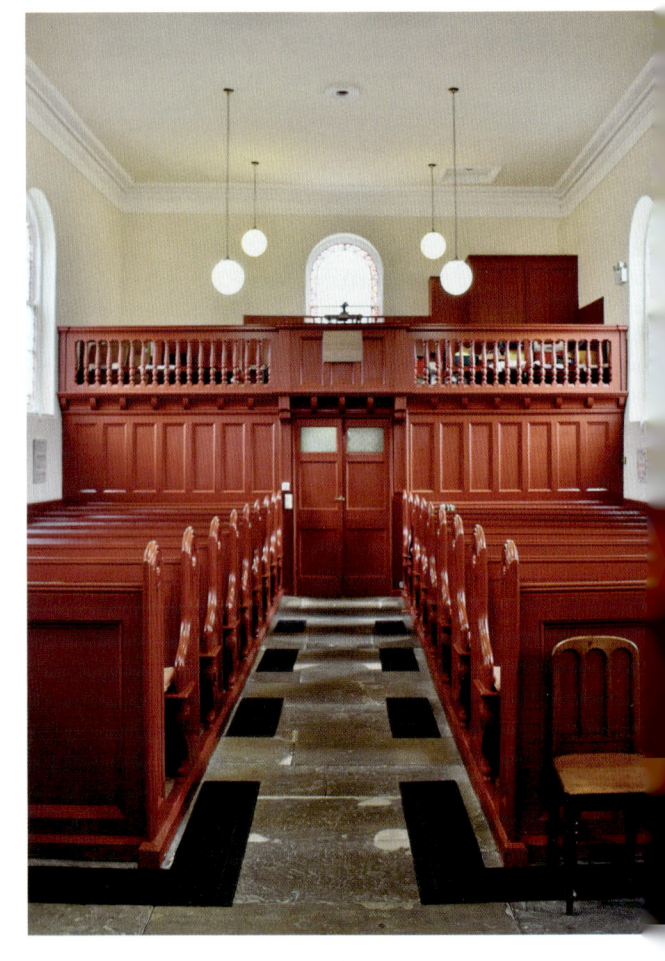

Despite being a landmark on St Saviourgate for over 300 years, the Unitarian Chapel is now seldom visited by those not in the congregation or interested in the recitals and concerts it holds. But inside and out, this church is a gem of architecture and history – it is the oldest non-conformist chapel in the city, one of many that sprung up in England in the 17th century.

Originally, St Saviourgate was a busy thoroughfare used by travellers leaving and entering the city. However, after Stonebow was built in front of St Saviourgate, it became an almost silent passageway and the chapel was hidden from view. The front of the chapel is an impressive display of symmetry, with two perfectly aligned trees framing the uniform brick building. This satisfying but modest aesthetic was all supposed to contribute to the non-conformist identity. Instead of being designed in the shape of a Latin cross with one longer arm at the bottom, as was the preferred floorplan for most churches, the Unitarian Chapel has all sections equal, more comparable to a Greek cross. The gates at the entrance were added in 1860 – they replaced a high wall which was intended to ward off any attacks against the dissenters. Inside you will find bright scarlet Victorian pews dating from the 1870s and wall carvings memorialising the lives of key non-conformists who contributed time or wealth to the church and the city.

The chapel was built for York's religious dissenters in the 17th century in response to the 1662 Act of Uniformity, which re-introduced the prayer book to the Church of England and demanded consistent rules for worship. The project was led by non-conformist Minister Ralph Ward who had served time in jail for his non-conformist views. It was the first time in the city that Protestant dissenters had a communal location to worship – before this, ministers would have to preach at individual houses. The original Presbyterian congregation has since evolved into the current Unitarians of York.

THE ROCKET IN THE HISCOX BUILDING

The fastest rocket to have flown in Earth's atmosphere is in York

3 Peasholme Green, YO1 7PR

Although visitors are not allowed in the building of the Hiscox Insurance offices, the modernist glass walls allow passers-by to freely admire a very surprising and impressive decommissioned 12-metre rocket through the window.

This missile was one of eight machines to form part of an American–Russian collaborative project towards the end of the Cold War, and marked a scientific olive branch in the decades-long international space race. Going under the code name Kholod (meaning 'cold' in Russian) the project was an attempt to create a hypersonic propulsion machine using 'scramjets' powered by liquid hydrogen. For ten years it held the record for fastest atmospheric speed, but was ultimately decommissioned and sold at auction for just under £40,000 eventually moving to its current location in 2015.

The office itself is an impressive contemporary building, designed by the architect responsible for the London Gherkin. The interesting pattern that interlaces the bricks was inspired by Peasholm Green's 18th-century wool market, and creates a basket-weave pattern that would have been seen on wool items.

Even when York moves forward, it takes its history with it.

KINGS SQUARE – CASTLE

INSCRIPTION OF THE ANCIENT SOCIETY OF FLORISTS

Oldest florist society in the world

Barnitts, 26 Colliergate, YO1 8BW
ancientsocietyofyorkflorists.co.uk

Above the door of 26 Colliergate, a black and gold inscription reads: 'On this site in 1768, The Ancient Society of York Florists held their first flower show. Happiness being the ultimate end proposed by the Society'.

The Ancient Society of York Florists is the oldest florist society in the world, and their 'first flower show' described on the plaque soon turned into an annual event which became the longest-running horticultural event in the world (even if the *Guinness Book of World Records* has yet to acknowledge them). The ultimate aim of the society, as is written on the plaque, was 'happiness' which they believed could be achieved through the cultivation of flowers.

When the society shows started, it was a very exclusive club. Only a true florist (who grew, rather than sold, flowers) was able to compete in the annual shows. As the fashions for flowers changed, so did the openness of the society. After the Second World War, the upper classes became less involved in the shows, allowing more 'everyday' gardeners and allotment owners the chance to demonstrate their horticultural prowess. And so the society continues, organising four events a year for hopeful competitors of all ages and abilities to go for that flowery gold prize.

ST ANDREW'S DRILL HALL

Headquarters of the First West Yorkshire Rifle Volunteer Battalion

St Andrewgate, YO1 8BH

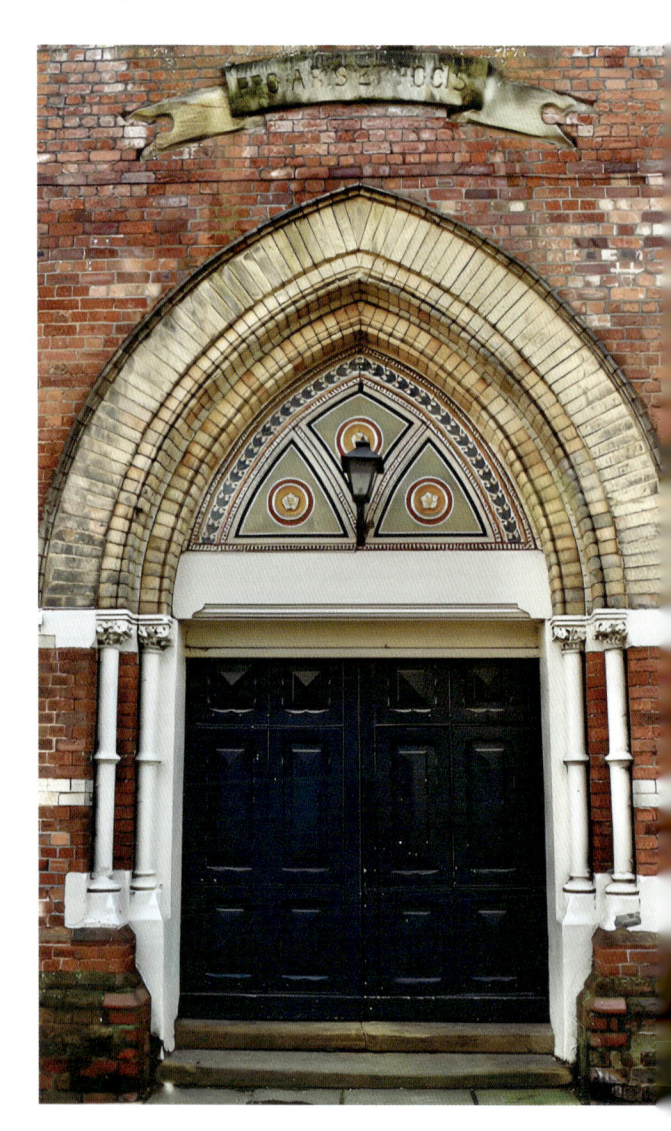

The unusual exterior design of St Andrew's Drill Hall (now the back entrance of Barnitt's homestore) is a beautiful example of 19th-century Neo-Gothic architecture, something not common around York. Yet, not many people venture down the quiet residential street of St Andrewgate to see it.

Beginning as a house in the early 19th century, the building was redesigned in 1872 as a headquarters for military use by a local firm, Gould and Fisher. Drill Halls became popular in the mid-19th century. They provided a space for the territorial army – the volunteer army reserves – to train together. They also acted as sites for socialising during community events such as dances and fairs when the volunteers weren't performing drills.

St Andrew's was used by the First West Yorkshire Rifle Volunteer Battalion for drills, admin and socials. Although the interior is now part of Barnitt's homestore, the exterior remains as intact as it was in 1872.

The banner above the door reads *Pro aris et focis* – Latin that translates as 'for altars and hearths' – to remind the Battalion what they would be fighting for if war ever came.

ROMAN BATH MUSEUM

A hidden basement museum

The museum of the Roman Bath Pub
9 St Sampson's Square, YO1 8RN
Monday–Thursday noon–5pm, Friday to Sunday 11am–4pm

Inside the entrance of The Roman Bath pub on St Sampson's Square is a staircase leading down into the remains of an original Roman bathhouse. As well as the excavated bathhouse, the museum displays artefacts and information on what the City of York would have been like over 2,000 years ago.

The bathhouse was built for a Roman military legion at some point during the Roman occupation of York, when the city was a fortress called Eboracum, some time between 71 and 122 AD. The military spa was fully equipped with the latest bathing technology – including ancient hot tubs – all designed in the classic Roman style, exclusively for the use of Roman soldiers. There may have been a gym, a swimming pool and food store but these are still to be discovered somewhere underground.

Once the Romans left England for good, the baths were abandoned and eventually built over. They remained undiscovered until the 1930s when the previous pub (the Mail Coach Inn) went through renovations.

In addition to the impressive stone remains of the spa, the Yorkshire Museum by the river also exhibits a number of ancient items which were lost in these Roman baths, such as gold rings, beads and games counters. Many of these were discovered through the excavations of a preserved Roman sewage system nearby, into which the water from the baths would have flowed, basically making this area of the museum the lost property box of a 2,000-year-old leisure complex.

SIGNED BRICKS

The bricks of the Mission

29 Swinegate, YO1 8AZ

At 29 Swinegate, the bricks which make up the foundations of the Biltmore Bar and Grill are decorated with letters. Four hundred to be exact, which correspond to the initials of the members of York Central Mission's parish, who each paid seven shillings in 1910 to add their names to the foundation stones of the Central Mission's brand-new hall. Over 100 years later, the names are still there, even if the Mission has since moved on.

York Central Mission is an independent branch of Methodism, a movement organised by John Wesley in the 18th century. This movement increasingly gained traction in York and the first Methodist church was built in the city in 1759 following a visit from Wesley himself. The new hall on Swinegate was acquired in the early 1900s, with enough space for a lecture hall, classrooms and community space. But despite the congregation making their mark all over the building, it was only used as a church for a few years. The space was soon needed for the war effort, and after the First World War ended, the Central Mission integrated with the Monk Bar Methodist Chapel. They quickly moved to a new location in Monkgate, leaving only their initials behind.

Where do the names Swinegate and Grape Lane come from?

Swinegate was named after the pigs (or swine) that were once brought to market and sold in this area of Roman York. The name of Grape Lane has evolved over the years, originally being a more explicit version of Grope Lane, referring to the place that people would go to find a lady of the night. Both pigs and prostitutes have not been seen here for a few hundred years, but the street names endure as a strong reminder of Ye Olde York.

THE COUNCIL CHAMBER
Political matters

The Courtyard, Coney Street, Y01 9QN
yorkconferences.com/venues/the-guildhall-york
Check website for open days

Upstairs in York's 15th-century replica Guildhall, overlooking the river through large windows, is York Council's private chamber. A distinguished and fitting place to conduct political affairs or commercial meetings, the room is rented out privately and so hardly features in York's public historical tours.

The chamber's walls are painted green, embellished with gold-leafed crowns and lions, disrupted by an imposing marble fireplace. It contains 4 leather-lined, wood-panelled seats which are often occupied by the council as it discusses local business.

The foundation stone of the council chamber was laid in 1889 and the whole room was finished two years later. Originally designed for the city council, it has since been used by many organisations for various reasons, but it still evokes an atmosphere of serious political decision-making. The ovular seating arrangement encourages equal, democratic discussion, and the larger throne-like chair at the south end is reserved for the Lord Mayor, who oversees the room on a raised platform.

Despite the sombre style of its 19th-century romantic Gothic decoration, the chamber has adapted with the times. Little divots in the oak desks, once used for inkwells, have been replaced with microphones, and voting buttons have been added.

Guildhall

The original Guildhall was constructed between 1449 and 1459 as a place for the Guilds of York to meet and agree the rules and regulations of trade. The building was supposed to signify the Guilds' wealth and power; masons used stone, rather than wood, to build the hall, and the ten magnificent timber pillars in the great hall were each made from a single oak tree trunk taken from the ancient royal Forest of Galtres. The Guildhall that stands there now is a replica, rebuilt in a sympathetic medieval style in the 1950s after the ceiling was bombed during the Baedeker air raids in the Second World War.

COLUMN
OF THE GEORGE INN

The grandest inn in the city

17 Coney Street, YO1 9QL

A single white column standing at the side of a street is not usually something to stop and look at, but the one on Coney Street has a wonderful history that makes it a fascinating, but unknown and unappreciated, symbol of York. Its story, which begins in 1455, involves elite businessmen, travellers from afar and even the Brontë sisters.

Hospicium Georgii was first mentioned in 1455 in a will belonging to the Chancellor of Exeter Cathedral. One hundred years later the George Inn was being managed by wealthy members of the upper classes of York, such as the Sheriff, Thomas Kaye, who himself took over from John Bilbowe, the Chamberlain of the city. The inn was originally elaborately decorated, with an ornate entrance and ecclesiastical carvings all along the walls, but by the 18th century it had been remodelled into a more subtle Georgian style, with only seven white pillars and a plain brick frontage.

Over the centuries the George Inn hosted countless travellers to the city. It is mentioned in the 17th- and 18th-century writings of John Taylor and York historian Francis Drake (not to be confused with the famous explorer), and was thought of at the time as the grandest inn in the city. Because of this, it hosted the crème de la crème of notable society, including architect Sir John Vanbrugh, diarist John Byng and authors Charlotte and Anne Brontë. As well as private rooms, the George Inn had a banqueting hall and spaces used for auctions, plays, dances, dog and horse markets and audits. In 1869, the building was demolished to make way for a new department store. The one white pillar is now all that remains of the prestigious George Inn.

BETTYS' MIRROR

⑰

Diamond carvings

Bettys Café, 6 St Helen's Square, YO1 8QP
bettys.co.uk
Daily 9am–5pm

The cakes and teas are so famous at Bettys that in all the excitement and sugar-rush the mirror in the basement corridor is hardly appreciated. Carved into this mirror are the names and signatures of over 600 people, chiselled into the glass during the Second World War. It is hard to imagine the classic Bettys Tea House as a hotspot for off-duty soldiers, but for the Canadian pilots stationed at York Airfields during the war, that is exactly what it was.

Bettys back then was a very different place: it was a place to unwind on an occasional evening off, a much-needed break from the daily realities of the war. Soldiers would meet at Bettys (nicknamed The Dive) for cocktails, music and dancing. It is during this period that they began a tradition of carving their names on the mirror behind the bar.

No one quite knows how the tradition started, though it is thought that the first inscription was created by an airman who had recently proposed to his girlfriend and used the diamond of the engagement ring to sign their names. The practice may have been encouraged by the owner, Frederick Belmont, so as to add to Bettys' interior décor. Belmont had based Bettys' interior on the famous luxury ocean liner HMS Queen Mary: he had sailed on the maiden voyage and loved the Art Deco design. The liner had apparently requested that all celebrity passengers sign their names in the guestbook, and it is possible that Belmont wanted to replicate the idea using the names of those he thought were the true celebrities of the age – the servicemen bravely fighting for the war effort.

A vast teapot collection

Displayed around all of Bettys' five branches situated in the North of England are items from the vast teapot collection which has been accumulating since Bettys opened in the 1930s. The York café has chosen to display the silver and silver-plated teapots in a glass case by the windows, in keeping with the décor of the branch.

THE MANSION HOUSE CAT

The cat mummy

St Helen's Square, YO1 9QL
mansionhouseyork.com
See website for opening times

Concealed behind a large painting of King George IV in the State Room of the Lord Mayor's city residence is the perfectly preserved skeleton of a cat. The mummified body is found by unhooking the royal picture from the wall and swinging it open, revealing the cat sitting on some shelves set into the wall.

This cat was discovered in the floorboards of the upstairs apartment rooms (the ones that the Lord Mayor now lives in) during renovation work a few years ago. It is thought that the cat was once a pet who, after passing away, was buried in the beams by the servants as a spiritual gesture – perhaps to protect the house, or to ease the departing of the cat's soul. Once discovered, the skeleton was brought downstairs to be displayed as part of the quirky history of the house. In 2015, there was an open competition to give the deceased pet a new name, and on Halloween night the cat was officially named Moggy Mortis.

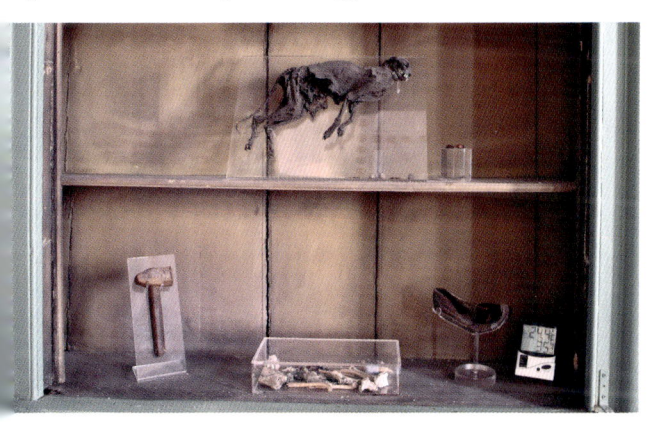

The bright Victorians

Looking out onto St Helen's Square, with Bettys, Stonegate and the Minster all in one vista, the Mansion House State Room offers one of the most picturesque views of the city. The huge interior is also impressively decked out with enormous portraits of mayors and kings, all hanging from the room's rich green walls. Historical investigation has found that this particular room has undergone 18 redecorations since it was first built. A variety of colours have adorned the room, but the most outrageous was the design chosen by the Victorians, who decided to cover every corner in bright pink paint and sparkling gold embellishment – a terrible choice for the guests who had to ensure their outfits did not clash with the walls.

Map of York

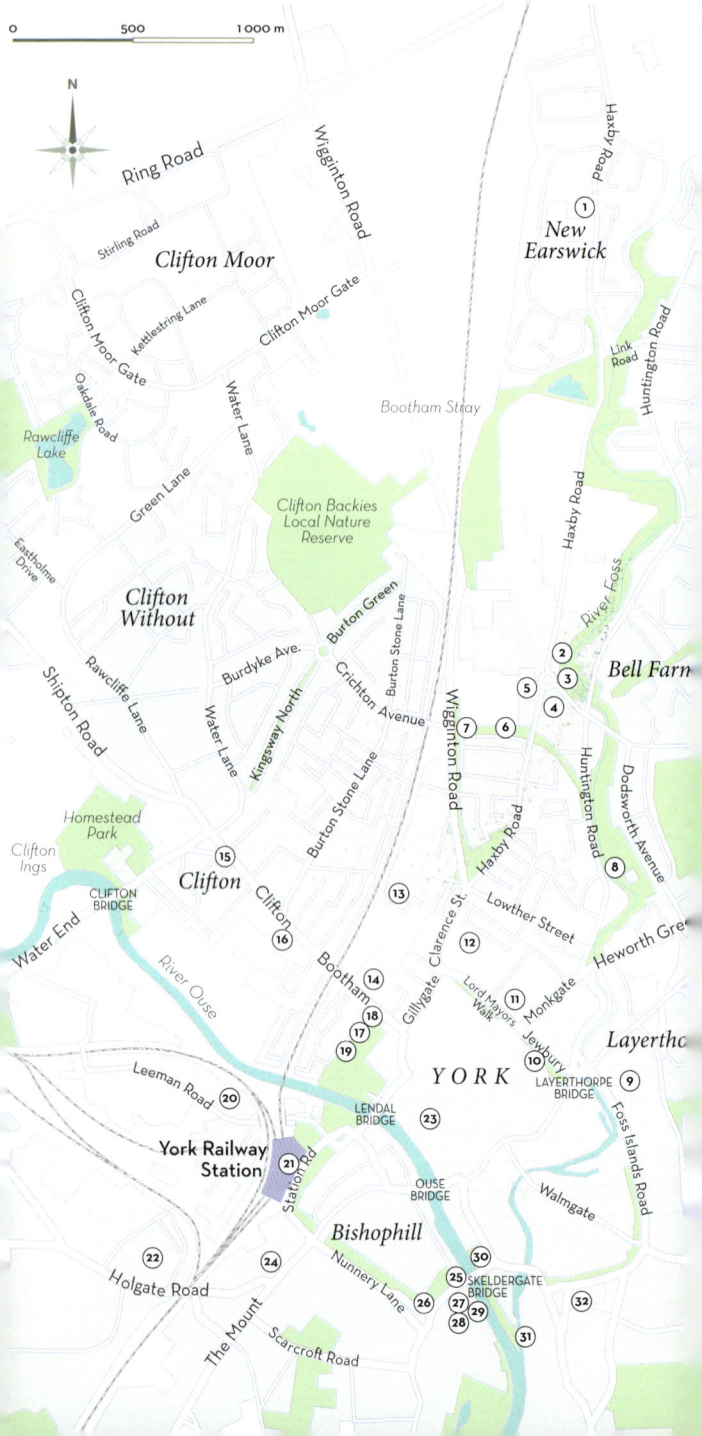

Scale: 0 — 500 — 1 000 m

N (compass)

Locations and Streets

- Ring Road
- Stirling Road
- Clifton Moor
- Wigginton Road
- New Earswick
- Haxby Road (Pear Tree)
- Kettlestring Lane
- Clifton Moor Gate
- Clifton Moor Gate
- Water Lane
- Link Road
- Huntington Road
- Oakdale Road
- Rawcliffe Lake
- Green Lane
- Bootham Stray
- Haxby Road
- Eastholme Drive
- Clifton Backies Local Nature Reserve
- River Foss
- Bell Farm
- Clifton Without
- Burdyke Ave.
- Burton Green
- Burton Stone Lane
- Crichton Avenue
- Rawcliffe Lane
- Shipton Road
- Water Lane
- Kingsway North
- Wigginton Road
- Haxby Road
- Huntington Road
- Dodsworth Avenue
- Homestead Park
- Clifton Ings
- Clifton Bridge
- Clifton
- Bootham
- Burton Stone Lane
- Heworth Green
- Water End
- River Ouse
- Clarence St.
- Lowther Street
- Gillygate
- Lord Mayor's Walk
- Monkgate
- Jewbury
- Layerthorpe
- Leeman Road
- Layerthorpe Bridge
- YORK
- Foss Islands Road
- York Railway Station
- Lendal Bridge
- Station Rd
- Ouse Bridge
- Walmgate
- Bishophill
- Nunnery Lane
- Skeldergate Bridge
- Holgate Road
- The Mount
- Scarcroft Road

Numbered Locations

1 — New Earswick
2, 3, 4, 5 — Bell Farm area
6, 7
8 — Dodsworth Avenue
9 — Layerthorpe
10 — Jewbury
11 — Monkgate
12 — Clarence St.
13
14 — Bootham
15, 16 — Clifton
17, 18, 19
20 — Leeman Road
21 — Station Rd
22
23 — Lendal Bridge
24
25, 26, 27, 28, 29, 30 — Skeldergate Bridge / Bishophill
31
32

Clifton – New Earswick

①	ALL SAINTS CHURCH	*128*
②	NEW EARSWICK	*130*
③	AERODROME MEMORIAL	*132*
④	YEARSLEY SWIMMING POOL'S INSCRIPTION	*134*
⑤	ROMAN ROCK	*135*
⑥	JOSEPH ROWNTREE THEATRE	*136*
⑦	MEMORIAL LIBRARY	*137*
⑧	HAXBY ROAD FOOTPATH	*138*
⑨	*THE BIG BLUE PIPE* SCULPTURE	*140*
⑩	MANHOLE COVER WITH PULLEYS	*141*
⑪	THE DESTRUCTOR	*142*
⑫	ICE HOUSE	*143*
⑬	BILE BEANS	*144*
⑭	PEACE GARDEN	*146*
⑮	BOOTHAM PARK HOSPITAL	*148*
⑯	BOOTHAM SCHOOL ASSEMBLY HALL	*140*
⑰	FORMER ELECTROBUS STATION	*150*
⑱	THE RECEPTION OF ST PETER'S SCHOOL	*152*
⑲	WOODEN SHUTTERS	*154*
⑳	ST MARY'S TOWER	*155*
㉑	ST OLAVE'S CHURCHYARD	*156*
㉒	SEARCH ENGINE	*158*
㉓	THE YORK ZERO POST	*159*
㉔	ST PAUL'S SQUARE	*160*
㉕	THE PRIESTS' HOLE OF THE SECRET CHAPEL	*162*
㉖	THE PROTECTED ODEON SIGN	*163*
㉗	BAILE HILL	*164*
㉘	BITCHDAUGHTER TOWER	*165*
㉙	GAME	*165*
㉚	HENRY RICHARDSON'S MEMORIAL	*166*
㉛	THE NUNNERY WALL	*168*
㉜	THE INSCRIPTION OF THE WATERFRONT HOUSE BAKERY	*170*
㉝	FLOOD BOARD	*172*
㉞	FOSSGATE BARRIER	*173*
㉟	PUBLIC VEGETABLE BED	*174*

ALL SAINTS CHURCH

A charming little-known country church

Church Lane, Huntington, YO32 9RE
huntingtonparish.org.uk
Opening times on website

The seasons arrive with style at All Saints Church, Huntington. In the early months of the year the graveyard is covered with the white spots of snowdrops, replaced by daffodils in the spring, and a firework of colour as summer comes. The church's miniature landscape, with rolling fields surrounding it and the River Foss flowing nearby, is so picturesque that it has been on the cover of many local magazines. Yet, three miles outside the city, it still remains little known by those who stick to the urban hum of York.

The best view comes when you cross over the bridge from the village and see the top of the church spire rise out from the tree canopy. Although most of this church dates back to a Victorian reconstruction, the original All Saints Church which stood on this spot in the 11th century would have had a tower where a lantern would be lit to guide people to the safety of the Church as they ventured through the ancient royal Forest of Galtres.

The interior of the church is not quite so beautiful as the outside, but there are interesting things to see if you know where to look. Of note is the stunning organ, built by Foster & Andrews of Hull for over £1,000 in the 1890s (around £100,000 today).

NEARBY

Tether rings

Exploring the gardens of All Saints Church is a treat in itself, but there are a few extra things to look out for among the graves and the flowers. Hanging on the brick walls to the left of the church entrance are iron tether rings, ready for any parishioners who rode to the service on horseback.

NEW EARSWICK

The model village

Hawthorn Terrace, YO23 4AQ
Bus 1 to New Earswick shops

About two miles north of the city centre is the village of New Earswick. At first glance it looks like any other mini suburb outside any other city in the UK, but after a while New Earswick starts to feel slightly eerie. Mostly because everything seems carefully curated to look exactly the same.

New Earswick is what is known as a model village. Built along strict aesthetic guidelines, it was supposed to be a sort of utopia for the working classes, in contrast to the increasing number of poverty-stricken slums appearing in the city. The confectioner Joseph Rowntree bought 150 acres of land near his chocolate factory in the early 1900s with the aim of creating affordable and attractive housing for the working-class citizens of York.

Rowntree wanted to foster a sense of social mobility: he encouraged both workers and managers to move into the new homes, as well as families who were not connected to the factory at all. It was an attempt to create a fully sustainable community, as opposed to one that lived off charity – the tenants paid a reasonably low rent, but the town planners still made a small profit from the village. Rowntree hired the architect Raymond Unwin to fill New Earswick with picture perfect houses, complete with vegetable beds and two fruit trees per family. All the village streets were named after trees, and following Rowntree's Quaker beliefs Unwin also ensured there were no pubs or bars built on site which might tempt the residents and ruin the pleasant atmosphere.

The community are more lenient than they once were: previously there were strict rules about what you could plant in the garden, or even what colour your door could be, but now you can plant what you like and new houses in new styles are being built around the area. And yet New Earswick still has a very self-contained, village atmosphere, which is rather unusual nowadays, especially in a place so close to a city centre. The Folk Hall exemplifies New Earswick's communal purpose – it is a hub of all things social, religious and operational in the village, and hosts numerous events and activities which anyone can get involved in. These have ranged from arts and crafts lessons to Pink Floyd concerts. It also has a post office, library and café so, unless you fancy a pint, once you are in New Earswick there really is no need to ever leave …

AERODROME MEMORIAL

③

In memory of the RAF and Handley Page personnel

Kettlestring Lane, Clifton, YO30 4XF

The chaotic centre of a sprawling industrial estate is not the place you would expect to find a heartfelt war memorial. The Aerodrome Memorial – a stone podium with a metal plaque bordered by plastic poppies – is made all the more difficult to find because it is below knee height, in a place dominated by large, towering buildings. It's worth hunting out though, if only to honour the fascinating group of Yorkshire men and women who worked on the Clifton Airfield before the outbreak of the Second World War.

Specifically, this memorial is dedicated to the RAF and Handley Page personnel and original members of the Yorkshire Aviation Services who operated the aerodrome between 1936 and 1939. The aerodrome was bought by the York Corporation in 1936, and was basically a civilian-run airport, used mostly for air-taxis and a flying club. From the 1920s, the national government had been encouraging local councils to start constructing their own airfields, and York became one of many cities to boast a municipal aerodrome. The Clifton Airfield, as it was known, was managed by Yorkshire Air Services and Country Club Ltd until 1939 when the government took back ownership for the sake of the war effort.

Clifton Airfield became an RAF site used for building and holding military machinery including Whitley Bombers, Westland Lysander, North American Mustang and Handley Page Halifax planes – a four-engine heavy bomber developed in the lead-up to the war. Throughout the war, the site was attacked and bombed, with personnel in constant danger.

Once the war had been won, the Handley Page Halifax bombers were decommissioned, and an industrial estate began to rise from the ashes of the airfield site. The area now covers almost all of what used to be York's aerodrome, leaving the Aerodrome Memorial to commemorate Clifton's role in the war.

YEARSLEY SWIMMING POOL'S INSCRIPTION ④

The only leisure pool in history to have been powered by fruit pastilles

Hayley's Terrace, YO31 8SB
Bus 1 or 5 to Nestlé Rowntree

Founded in 1908 by the confectioner Joseph Rowntree, Yearsley Swimming Baths might be the only leisure pool in history to have been powered by fruit pastilles: the pool itself was heated by steam that was generated by the Rowntree factory (which later became part of Nestlé) through a tunnel that went under Haxby Road.

The very first Yearsley Bath was less formally constructed than the current one. It was part of the River Foss, next door to where the present building stands, and consisted of a brick floor, wire netting across the river to mark off the pool area, stone steps down into the water and two wooden huts for changing. It was fit for purpose but probably dangerous, and definitely on the chilly side, so when Rowntree offered to build the new Yearsley Baths, the river pool was removed.

Rowntree was already a well-known and admired philanthropist by this point and his generous gift of a public swimming pool (donated to the City of York for community use in 1909) was gratefully received by the local community. It was described by contemporaries as 'the finest open-air swimming bath in Yorkshire'. Ladies and gentlemen swam on separate days, and children were allowed to go in for free, so as to practise 'the art of swimming'. Although the days of urban-river swimming were gone, the new Yearsley Bath still kept some of the magic of the outdoors, and the pool remained open-air until the 1960s, at which point a roof was added to the building.

Another project in the early 2000s saw £1m spent on a complete modernisation of the building. The Yearsley Baths prides itself on having the last Edwardian 50-yard swimming pool in the North of England, but the only visible part that still dates back to the original baths is the inscription built into the brickwork outside which marks the pool as a gift to the city.

NEARBY
Roman rock ⑤

In the front garden of the baths is a rock feature which has an unresolved mystery behind it. Local historians believe that this rock was used by the Romans to support a bridge over the River Foss, allowing people to easily cross the river and visit nearby camps. It is thought the rock came from further away and was brought over to this spot by a contraption that floated it down the river, but there are still many unanswered questions around the source, transportation and use of this mysterious Yearsley rock.

JOSEPH ROWNTREE THEATRE ⑥

A theatre for a full and happy life

Haxby Road, YO31 8TA
josephrowntreetheatre.co.uk
Bus 1, 5, 5a to Nestlé Rowntree

Compared to the grand Theatre Royal ostentatiously located in the centre of town, the small brick frontage of the Joseph Rowntree Theatre is completely hidden: it is found in a quiet part of York, behind thick foliage and narrow gates.

But its hidden location and modest appearance make the dynamic events going on inside even more appealing – this is a theatre that was made for the community, and the community still owns it.

The theatre was created in the 1930s for Rowntree's factory workers. It often functioned as a cinema as well as a theatre, and at lunchtime the employees of the factory would go there via an underground passage for 20 minutes of rest and relaxation before heading back to work. Rowntree was a dedicated Quaker and (considering the Quakers' disapproval of frivolous entertainment) this may have been the only Quaker-funded theatre in the world.

The Art-Deco design was state of the art and was distinctly modern compared to the grand Victorian theatres of previous generations. Over time the building has seen a few small renovations, but nearly all of the original structure remains.

The theatre is now managed by a board of trustees, but it is run by a team of passionate volunteers who organise up to six performances a week without any paid staff, motivated by their love of the arts. Professional productions are rare, and it is mostly community groups which grace the stage, ranging from dance performances, live music, tribute bands, pantomimes and musicals: if you want to see the creative side of York, this is where to find it.

There are plans to expand the small theatre and add some additional facilities (bar, café and extra rehearsal space), but the original building will keep its Art-Deco charm and continue promoting the general ethos of public engagement.

The directors still abide by Seebohm Rowntree's original purpose for the hall, namely to create a centre that promotes 'recreational and educational activities which make for a full and happy life'.

NEARBY
Memorial library (7)
Haxby Rd, York YO31 8TA

The intriguing little building fronting the enormous old chocolate factory was once the Joseph Rowntree Memorial Library. It was opened in 1927 for the Rowntree employees and, although it is now empty of books and closed to visitors, it remains a Grade II listed building because of its panels, cupboards and – crucially – the original umbrella rack.

HAXBY ROAD FOOTPATH

The intoxicating smell of chocolate

Just off Haxby Road, Clifton, YO31 8JJ

The whole length of the enormous factory owned by Nestlé Confectionery can be seen from the pavement of Haxby Road, but is not a very inspiring view – it is certainly no Willy Wonka's. To make the most out of the sweetest corner of York, you need to take a stroll down the footpath that runs underneath Haxby Road. You can see the old Rowntree factory from here but more importantly, due to the location, wind and chocolatey magic, this short section of the Foss Island Cycle Route is often completely enveloped in the overwhelming aroma of roasted cocoa beans. You can even follow the scent through the @YorkChocAroma twitter account which not only gives the location of the best smells but identifies the flavours in the air including peppermint, sugar and cocoa.

This footpath lies near to both the Nestlé factory and the Cargill plant which produces a cocoa liquor for food manufacturers. The combined efforts of these businesses result in a massive amount of chocolate production in the area: every day, the York Nestlé factory makes 7 million bars of chocolate, including Aeros, Milkybars, Yorkies and KitKats.

Before Nestlé took over Rowntree Macintosh Ltd in 1988, the factory was the Rowntree production headquarters. Despite the potential for a characterless manufacturing hub, Rowntree's focus was always on creating a good working environment for the employees. The site had landscaped gardens, employee benefits and even ornamental planting. The production areas themselves contributed to a feeling of well-being, because who would not be happy working in the Cream Block or the Cake Department?

Nestlé continued the work of Rowntree's and is now the largest private employer in York with 2,000 employees.

A unique 100% English chocolate

The cocoa plant is notoriously difficult to grow in the English climate: it much prefers the South American tropics or West African heat. In fact, the only successful chocolate bar to have been completely produced on English soil came from York's Rowntree factory in 1932, using sugar, vanilla and cocoa made from a cocoa plant grown in the factory's hothouse.

It was given to the then Princess Elizabeth, who can claim to be the only person in the world to have eaten a 100% English bar of chocolate.

THE BIG BLUE PIPE SCULPTURE

Not the usual industrial pipe ...

Foss Island Cycle Path, opposite Clifton Allotments
Crichton Avenue, YO31 8JG

One of the least well-known of York's hidden attractions is a long, winding and unpredictable blue steel pipe which starts at the beginning of a footpath in Clifton and follows the Foss Island Cycle route all the way to its end in Derwenthorpe.

Cropping up randomly in different guises, the blue pipe seems to appear from underground. It is a complete mystery to those who only see parts of it along the route: in order to really appreciate it, it is far better to hop on a bike and do the whole tour.

Far from being just an industrial pipe, this is actually one long connected piece of art. The sculpture (officially called *The Big Blue Pipe*) was commissioned by Sustrans, a walking and cycling company who created the National Cycling Network.

Originally this route was part of a local railway track, but once this became disused, Sustrans acquired the route and made it part of their national cycle path. They like to add pieces of public art and focus points along the journey to keep it interesting.

The Big Blue Pipe was designed in the 1990s by the sculptor George Cutts as an above-ground marker for the York Waterworks pipe which runs underneath the path, and once supplied the city with clean water.

It swirls and loops, changes size and even forms itself into objects. Although the pipe has accumulated quite a lot of wear and tear over the years, and the blue paint is now covered in graffiti, it remains an impressive piece of art. It livens up any cycle ride and turns a potentially dull footpath into a game of hide and seek.

NEARBY

Manhole cover with pulleys (10)

The Big Blue Pipe is not the only mystery along this path. Further on towards Tang Hall is an old Victorian manhole cover surrounded by five heavy machinery pulleys. It could be another piece of art, or it could have been part of the local railway track which once connected York to Selby, although what it would have been used for is now anybody's guess.

THE DESTRUCTOR

A rubbish chimney

Foss Islands Road, Layerthorpe, YO31 7UJ

Stand at any spot in the Fossgate area and the focal point of the skyline will always be a giant brick chimney, 55 metres tall, weighing 2,120 tonnes, and which has the best name that any piece of industrial equipment could hope for: the Destructor. 'Destructor' was the original name given to incinerators (machines which dispose of rubbish and waste) when the invention was patented in 1874. The one on Foss Islands Road was put up in the late 19th century in an attempt to clean up the city by resolving York's mounting rubbish problem. The waste would go in and industrial black smoke would come out.

Alongside the tower, there also used to be a coal-fired power plant which generated electricity for the city. Being slightly conspicuous, the whole plant had to be camouflaged during World War II: one of the cooling towers was completely covered in tar and the Destructor was treated to an army-style operational-camouflage paint job to ensure that it would not be spotted during the nightly air raids. The power plant survived the Blitz only to be partly blown up a few years after the war had ended due to an undetected crack in one of the steel boilers.

Most of the remaining parts of the plant were taken down in the 1970s and York now burns its waste at Allerton Park instead, but the tower became a Grade II listed building and consequently cannot be moved. It has now been nicknamed 'the Morrisons' Chimney since the supermarket chain moved in next door

- 142 -

CLIFTON – NEW EARSWICK

ICE HOUSE

The Georgian freezer

*Along the wall starting from Monk Bar, Goodramgate
Or accessed through the garden of the Keystones Pub, 4 Monkgate, YO31 7PE*

Before the days of fridges and freezers, keeping things cold was a little difficult.

Ice was the obvious answer, but the problem was how to stop it melting. The Georgians came up with a solution: ice houses. One of these brick caves, designed to keep ice frozen throughout the year, can be found hiding next to the City Walls, along the path near the Monkgate entrance.

This ice house was probably built around 1800, for either a nearby public house or a local wealthy family of wine merchants who used it to keep their drinks cool throughout the summer months. The exposed brick makes it look a bit run-down, but this would not have mattered when it was first built because ice houses were originally covered in earth and grass, thus completely camouflaged in their surroundings. Inside, a deep pit was cold enough to store the ice until the owners needed it.

The first ice houses appeared in Britain in the early 17th century. The ice was first cut from frozen water by ice hackers who worked on local rivers or canals during the winter. They would bring these slabs of ice to the ice houses to be stored until summer, when demand for cold food and drinks would peak. With the growth of international shipping, eventually the ice began to arrive into York from as far away as the lakes of Norway. Ice houses were mostly used by affluent families who wanted to be able to offer their guests chilled drinks and cool food all year round. They were a status symbol up until the turn of the 20th century when refrigerators were invented, which meant that the ice houses were no longer needed.

Once the ice trade melted away in the 20th century, the function of these ice houses started to evolve. They are still scattered around the country and have been used as air raid shelters, fruit stores, wine cellars and even garden sheds.

BILE BEANS

Ghost advertisement

18 Lord Mayor's Walk, YO31 7ER

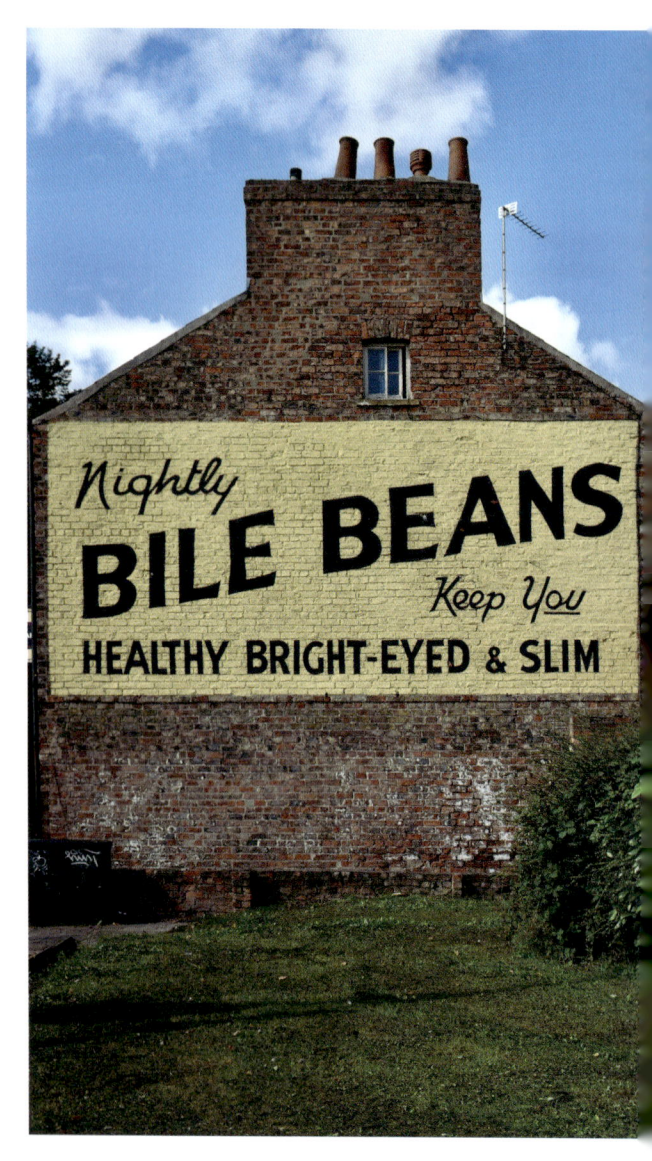

Before the days of targeted pop-up internet ads, a painted advert on the side of a shop or house was a clever way of getting local attention for various goods and services. York still has a few ghost advertisements dotted around, and the advert for Bile Beans, which has been there since the 1940s, continues to be repainted every now and then despite the fact that production of the product stopped in the 1980s. It is even more surprising that production lasted that long, given that Bile Beans were exposed as an elaborate fraud 70 years earlier.

Bile Beans were supposed to cure you of every medical ailment you could possibly succumb to: flu, dizziness, the 'female weakness' would all disappear after taking one of these magic beans. According to the official press, this was because of the secret scientific concoction in the beans, known only to Aboriginal Australians who had perfected the ability to live without illness. The owners of the Bile Beans Manufacturing Company, Charles Fulford and Ernest Gilbert, also invented a fictional scientist called Charles Ford who was said to have found and perfected the secret bean formula.

The fabricated tale was told through a £60,000 marketing campaign in the early 1900s (around £7m in today's money) which exaggerated the medical abilities of Bile Beans through national newspapers, posters, puzzles, a cookbook and even a song. These claims were exposed as fraudulent after the owners tried to sue another competitor for using the name Bile Beans. They were instead told that they could not have legal ownership of the name because the product did not really exist, and was entirely based on lies. Despite this exposé, the beans remained popular and the company went from strength to strength.

The company's marketing strategy slyly followed the fashions, and by the 1940s it had become a fat loss tablet aimed at women, appealing to the new slimming trend. This is when a house-owner in York decided to sell his wall to keep the ghost sign, and Bile Beans were forever immortalised as a product to keep you 'healthy, bright-eyed and slim'.

Advert: Medically approved Bile Beans. Wellcome Collection

PEACE GARDEN

A garden to commemorate a world free from nuclear war

St John's University Campus, Lord Mayor's Walk, YO31 7EX
Daily 8am–5pm

Hidden in the middle of York's oldest higher education institution, under the shadow of a concrete chapel, is a small Japanese Peace Garden. Whenever the gates are unlocked, anyone can pop into the garden and enjoy a few minutes of calm and contemplation. The space was originally a traditional English rose garden. In 2005 it was transformed into a Japanese wonderland, with traditional features of raked gravel, stepping-stone paths and a central water feature using stone taken from the old gates of Lord Mayor's Walk.

There is a water basin at the entrance for cleansing, and a stone path that runs through the garden. Placed along the route are natural features (life obstacles) each specifically chosen for their beauty or symbolism and positioned so they can all be appreciated individually. Far from being just a typical well-being feature, this garden was deliberately created as a symbol of international peace and prosperity. The garden was designed around a single Chinese Parasol Tree (Firmiana platanifolia) which had been brought from Japan.

The Parasol Tree had been grown from the seeds of a Japanese Hibakujumoku (translated as 'survivor tree'), which is the name used for plants that had been exposed to atomic radiation when bombs were dropped onto the Japanese cities of Hiroshima and Nagasaki at the end of the Second World War. The sapling was donated to York St John University by the National Federation of University Co-operative Associations as part of an anniversary project to remember the world's first use of the atomic bomb. The project was designed to pass a love of peace and respect for living things to future generations and share with British people a vision of a world free from nuclear weapons'.

Unfortunately, the Parasol Tree thrives in tropical environments, and with York's freezing winters, the poor sapling did not make it long past its tenth birthday. Although the Parasol Tree is no longer there, the spirit of the plant lives on in the Japanese Cloud Tree that has taken its place.

BOOTHAM PARK HOSPITAL

The former York Lunatic Asylum

Bootham, YO30 7BY

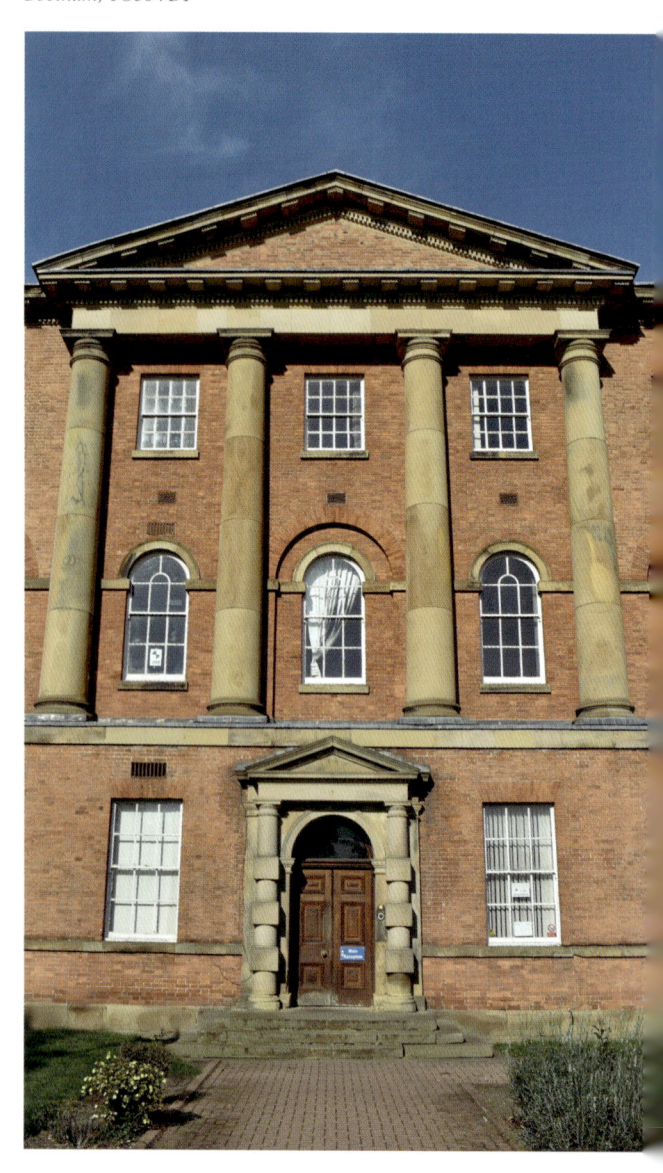

The grounds of an abandoned psychiatric hospital may sound like an eerie place to explore. Luckily, the old reception of Bootham Park Hospital (the former York Asylum) was designed to look more like a country manor than a stereotypical psychiatric facility, so unless you break into it at night it, is still a lovely place to look around even if the main building has been left empty for years.

York Asylum was one of the first in the country to try to create awareness of the mentally ill. A landscaped Palladian hall, designed in the 1770s by the famous architect John Carr, had plenty of space for recreational activities (including a bowling alley), all intended to improve the well-being of the patients.

Unfortunately, initial best intentions aside, the hospital soon ran into problems. It was discovered that within the beautiful Georgian building, many of the patients lived in horrendous conditions. The floors were covered in urine and excrement, the windows were too high to see out of, and one woman, Hannah Mills, died due to the terrible environment of the hospital.

It led to a national scandal, police investigations and a suspiciously timed fire, which led to most of the evidence going up in flames.

An Act of Parliament passed in 1854, the Lunacy Act, changed the status of the mentally ill from social outcasts to patients and the York Asylum was forced to clean up its act. The complex expanded in order to provide more space for the patients, and the governance of the organisation was reformed to prevent future corruption.

The Asylum evolved into an NHS psychiatric hospital and continued to treat patients until it closed in 2015. Although the building now backs onto York Hospital, the old Asylum has been empty ever since.

NEARBY
Bootham School Assembly Hall (16)
49-57 Bootham, YO30 7BU

Next to Bootham Park Hospital is the second Bootham School – the first Bootham School burned down in the late 19th century after one enthusiastic science pupil accidentally started a fire during a snail-burning experiment. In the rebuilding, an award-winning Assembly Hall was designed by Trevor Dannatt. Defined as 'brutalist', it used exposed concrete in a modernist post-war style. It is a pretty powerful building and, whether you love or hate the 1960s obsession with concrete, the Hall has now been listed as a protected building, so it is there to stay.

FORMER ELECTROBUS STATION ⑰

York, a city where electric buses were first introduced in 1915 ...

Clifton Green, Clifton, YO30 6BA
Bus 2 to Clifton Green

York is currently leading the charge to be the first zero-emissions city in Britain. By only allowing bikes and electric vehicles inside the walls, widening pavements and increasing the number of cycle lanes, it hopes to cut total carbon emissions to zero. Such forward-looking initiatives are perhaps surprising for a city better known for its ancient past, but this is not York's first foray into environmentally friendly transportation: the city has been experimenting in electric transport for quite some time. At the top of Clifton Green, a small brick building, although now empty, was built to charge the groundbreaking 'electrobuses' that were introduced to the city over 100 years ago.

Four battery-powered electric buses were bought in 1915 to ensure that the people living in the villages on the outskirts of the city could easily travel into and out of York. The buses could go 50 miles once fully charged and, under the terms of the operator's contract, they could hit a speedy 12mph.

Similar to today, the electric vehicles were pioneered as a fast, green and cheaper alternative to the petrol-guzzling automobiles and the slow horse-drawn buses; York became one of only eight towns in the country to operate these new electrobuses.

They were popular for a few years, but by the 1920s the buses had begun to grow tired. The batteries had become unreliable and needed constant charging, there was an inconsistent passenger demand, a lot of maintenance and most importantly a decline in profits.

Meanwhile, petrol buses were improving quickly. They could be bought and run more cheaply, and they were much more reliable. In 1921, the electrobus service to Clifton was removed, and the charging station found a new role as a public toilet and then as a barber. It is now in the market for a new identity.

York's association with electric vehicles recommenced in 2018 when the city became electrified again. Poppleton's Park and Ride became Britain's first all-electric Park and Ride route, and now visitors to York can take a ride on the world's first electric double-decker sightseeing bus.

THE RECEPTION OF ST PETER'S SCHOOL

An award-winning modern welcome

St Peter's School
Clifton, YO30 6AB
eventbrite.co.uk/o/st-peters-school-york-7300489187
Open for public lectures and open days

The fourth oldest school in the world, St Peter's School moved to its current location in Bootham in the 19th century. Because of its age, you would probably expect such an ancient institution to be housed in ancient bricks. Not so.

The first place you see when you get to the school is the award-winning reception building, one of the few pieces of modern architecture in York which successfully disguises itself, inside and out, as a natural part of an old building.

The finished interior won the Press People's Award in the annual York Design competition in 2014, impressing the judges with the combination of the exposed Victorian brick of the original walls and a brand-new contemporary glass roof. It is a genuinely beautiful architectural addition to an already impressive building and gives a visual indication that the old St Peter's is working to ensure it remains relevant in the modern world.

St Peter's School was founded in 627 AD by St Paulinus, who was also busy founding York Minster at this time. The school moved around a lot (the 'Peterites' seem to have occupied most corners of York at one time or another), but settled down in Bootham in the 1830s. St Peter's now occupies 47 acres of land that reaches right down to the river.

Infamous alumni

The most renowned past pupil of St Peter's was the infamous Guy Fawkes, who was caught trying to blow up the Houses of Parliament in 1605 as part of a Catholic plot to overthrow the Protestant throne. Although Fawkes was a pupil at St Peter's a long time before the school moved to its current location, the land that the school now stands on actually once belonged to the Fawkes Family. Although not condoning the actions of a religious extremist, St Peter's still refuses to burn a Guy Fawkes effigy like the rest of the country does as part of Bonfire Night on 5 November. Once a Peterite, always a Peterite.

WOODEN SHUTTERS

An ingenious but simple 13th-century defence mechanism

Marygate, YO30 7WZ

As you come out of the back entrance of the Museum Gardens and make your way up Marygate, keep an eye out for two obscure wooden shutters built high into the stone walls that run along the boundary of the old abbey. They are easy to miss, although at some point their location was made slightly more visible with the attachment of a now worn-out descriptive sign onto the wall at eye-level. This sign explains that the shutters are replicas of an ingenious, yet simple, 13th-century defence mechanism used by medieval archers to protect themselves from incoming invaders.

Bowmen would place themselves on the timber walkway behind the walls and shoot arrows at any attackers through the swinging shutters. The shutters would then quickly close and save them from any return fire. Although the shutters you can see in the walls are copies, the grooves that they slip into are original and thought to be the only ones left in the country.

Instead of protecting the city, these defences were built to fortify St Mary's Abbey. This section is clearly not as grand as the City Walls, and it took over 100 years for the abbey to be completely protected from all sides. Nevertheless, the occupiers of the abbey were very happy with their defences; not only were they protected from invaders, but they were also now shielded from any local people who attempted illegal access to the beautiful grounds.

NEARBY

St Mary's Tower (20)
Found at the end of Marygate

St Mary's Tower looks like an inconsequential part of the City Walls, but it played a key role in the English Civil War and many of its battle wounds can still be found scarred into its stone. In 1644, the Parliamentarians organised an attack on York (a Royalist city) in a battle which would come to be known as the Siege of York. They dug down under St Mary's Tower and used gunpowder to blow it up, causing enough damage to gain access to the Abbey. Fierce fighting then took place throughout the Abbey Gardens, until the Parliamentarians were finally driven back out the way they came in.

Following the end of the war, an attempt was made to repair the damage to the tower, in part using recycled materials: the door in St Mary's was taken from the King's Manor and the ground floor window once belonged to the Abbey. They fixed her up as best they could, but the damage from the attack can still be clearly seen in the holes and the cracks down the side of the wall.

ST OLAVE'S CHURCHYARD

A sanctuary of calm

8 Marygate Lane, YO30 7BJ
stolaveschurch.org.uk
To arrange to look around the churchyard
email churchwardens@stolaveschurch.org.uk
Church is open daily, see website for details

The fenced off St Olave's cemetery is locked away between the towering remains of St Mary's Abbey and the old Viking church of St Olave. Separated from the energetic picnic atmosphere of Museum Gardens, and particularly beautiful in the spring when the cherry blossoms are flowering, St Olave's small churchyard is a sanctuary of calm. It can only be accessed through the back door of the church when unlocked by St Olave's wardens, which means it is hardly ever occupied.

The dominant feature of the churchyard is the tomb of William Etty, the famous York artist. The imposing grave is situated at the top of the burial ground, overlooking all the other headstones. Much of the tomb's stonework has now crumbled, and there is a conservation effort led by the church to restore it.

Born the 7th child of a baker, Etty became a celebrated painter and eventually took commissions from Prince Albert. He was also a prominent local figure in his later years due to his campaigns to protect the city's medieval walls from demolition: his statue now stands outside York Art Gallery. As the *Yorkshire Gazette* wrote upon his death, 'Mr Etty was indeed a man of whom not only the City of York, but England as a nation, has a right to be proud'.

Considering Etty's national celebrity, it may seem odd to lay him to rest in the quiet and secluded churchyard of St Olave's. In fact, Etty had originally planned to be buried prestigiously in York Minster, but upon his death in 1849 it was discovered that he had failed to cover the cost of the extravagantly expensive Minster burial in his will. His friends decided the best option would be St Olave's so that he could still be close to the Minster, and the public were still able to pay their respects through the holes in the ancient abbey walls.

The Viking church

St Olave's is a rare example of a Nordic church – it was allegedly the first one in the whole of the British Isles dedicated to the first king and patron saint of Norway, Olaf Haroldsson. The church has undergone a few reconstructions, and most of what is here dates from the 15th century, although the 11th-century Viking foundations remain. It is thought that the founder of the church, a Scandinavian traveller-turned-politician called Siward, is buried somewhere in the churchyard, but no one quite knows where. A statue of St Olave (the Anglicised version of Olaf) stands above the main entrance to the church, holding a large cross to demonstrate his conversion from Paganism to Christianity.

SEARCH ENGINE

The secret life of trains

National Railway Museum
Leeman Road, YO26 4XJ
railwaymuseum.org.uk/research-and-archive/plan-research-visit
To visit, contact search.engine@railwaymuseum.org.uk
For opening times see website

Little known to the millions of visitors admiring the giant locomotives of the National Railway Museum are 25,000 books, 1m drawings, 11,000 posters, 2,300 prints, 1,000 paintings and 1,750,000 photographs relating to trains, engineering and travel that are held right underneath their feet. These collections comprise the Search Engine, the National Railway Museum's huge underground library and archive, which has been open to the public since 2008.

Going down into the basement archives is a museum experience all in itself. Each room (in a seemingly never-ending number of rooms) is designated by theme and filled with rows of files, boxes, books and paintings that can be taken up to the purpose-built research centre, examined and enjoyed. They are an important – but relatively unknown – extension of the famous museum upstairs, and just as crucial in narrating the railway history of the world.

The archive first appeared when the museum opened in 1975, but initially it was only home to the records of various railway companies. Through years of expansion the Search Engine has now accumulated some brilliant treasures – from detailed drawings of the very first engines and defensive railway plans in case of nuclear attack, to personal letters, such as one written by Charles Dickens to the Great Western Railway Company after losing his Christmas Turkey to a goods van fire.

NEARBY

The York 'zero' post

York Railway Station, Station Rd, York YO24 1AB

The York 'zero' post illustrates York's dominant role in the British railway mania' of the early 1800s. It marks the central point of ten North Eastern Railway Lines, all of which were connected to York's Railway Station. The one situated in the York Railway Station is a replica erected in 2004, but the original post would have been used to measure these railway lines and calculate the fares. Only 50 years after the first train left York in 1839 from a little wooden platform on Queen Street, the railway industry had grown enormously; by 1889, the new and magnificent York Railway station saw 300 trains going in and out of the city every day.

ST PAUL'S SQUARE

The horseshoe square

St Paul's Square, Holgate, YO24 4BD

Every city has a corner of affluence that stands a bit apart from the rest. This is St Paul's Square, the first and only formally laid out 'square' in York (although it is technically in the shape of a horseshoe). St Paul's is much the same today as it was when it was built in the 1850s, hidden from the main road by a narrow street, and centred around a private park cocooned by a sweeping row of impressive terraced houses. The original cast-iron railings and streetlamps in St Paul's Square are all still standing, and although you cannot see them, some of the houses still have remnants of private outdoor privies and coal houses in their back gardens – other examples of Victorian wealth.

Squares started to become fashionable in the 17th century. The new design allowed the upper middle classes to separate themselves from both the cramped terraced houses of the poor and the private country estates of the aristocracy. The square's purpose was to give a private outdoor space to the residents of the grand houses and to 'landscape' urban living. It was an interesting change from the idea that all space in the city had to be useful, through holding events and local markets, for example, and squares were associated with pleasure gardens, wealthy communities and status – leisure for leisure's sake.

For a long time, London was the only city that was wealthy enough to build squares, but through the 19th century this architectural fashion moved north. Even when it reached York, as St Paul's demonstrates, the square design continued to copy the style of the exclusive London homes in the areas of St George's, Berkeley, Mayfair and Belgravia.

St Paul's was an icon of York's status at the time, but by the end of the century, people were more interested in public parks than private squares, and there were no more squares built in the city. It was designated a protected area in the 1970s to ensure York's first and only venture into formal square construction would be preserved.

THE PRIESTS' HOLE OF THE SECRET CHAPEL

Ladies of the bar

17 Blossom Street, YO24 1AQ
bar-convent.org.uk
Monday–Saturday 10am–5pm

Behind the grand Georgian façade of 17 Blossom Street, an order of Catholic nuns hid for over 300 years, practising in an illegal convent. The architecture was deliberately designed to blend in with the surrounding buildings, all the while covering a magnificent domed chapel and a living space for the secret Catholic daughters of York.

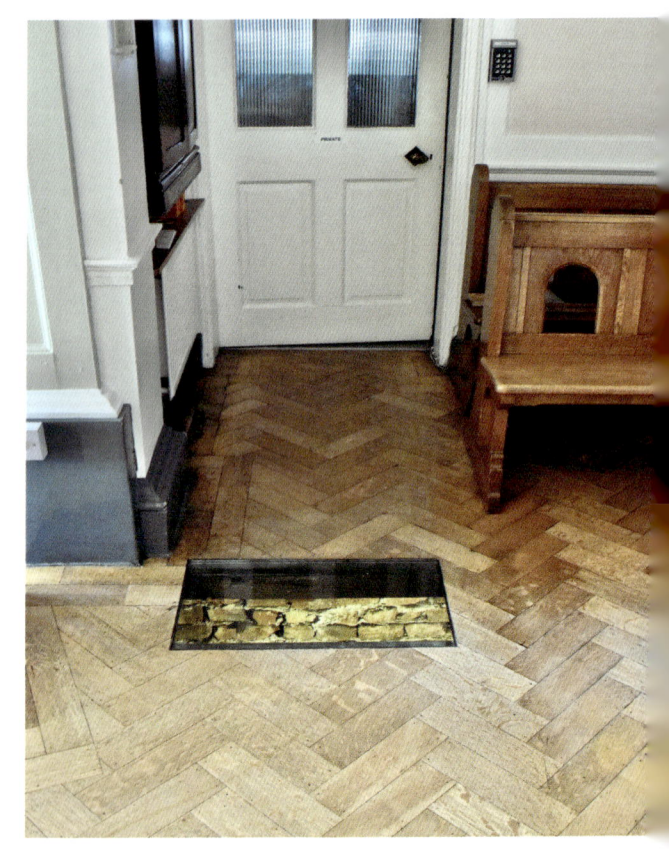

The Bar Convent is now a living heritage site where the sisters still practise, making it the oldest Catholic convent in England. Visitors are welcome, and an impressive permanent exhibition details its history.

Founded in secret in 1689 by a woman called Frances Bedingfield, the Bar Convent was part of a Catholic resistance movement that began when Catholicism was made illegal. It was opened to Catholic women as a school, church and home.

About 100 years after the convent was established, the mother superior at the time, Ann Aspinal, hired a local architect, Thomas Atkinson, to renovate the building. Catholicism was still illegal at this point, and Atkinson's main role was to ensure that their identity was kept a secret. He created a slate roof outside in order to cover the magnificent neo-classical dome of the secret chapel and built eight exits around the room to allow the nuns a quick escape route if the chapel was raided. Built into the floor is a priests' hole which leads to the underground room where the priest would have hidden in the event of a raid.

The chapel has interesting artefacts around its walls including the withered hand of Margaret Clitherow, a local legend who hid Catholic runaways in her house in the Shambles and was eventually crushed to death on the Ouse Bridge as a severe punishment for her religious crimes.

NEARBY

The protected Odeon sign

Everyman, Blossom St, YO24 1AJ

In an odd quirk of heritage, the cinema on Blossom Street might forever be confused as to which franchise it is working for. Despite now being an Everyman cinema, signage for the Odeon can also be seen pinned to the wall. This is because the site, which was the first Odeon in York and the oldest surviving cinema in the city, is a protected historic building and the Odeon sign cannot be removed. Font-lovers might notice that the style of writing is different from Odeon's recognisable branding. When the cinema was built in 1937, the council demanded that the striking Art Nouveau cinema change the font to conform to the aesthetic of the city.

BAILE HILL

The 'other' hill

City Walls, Skeldergate, YO1 6DT

Poor Baile Hill has been overlooked by its more famous twin for almost 1,000 years. While Clifford's Tower features as the unequivocal landmark of the city, Baile Hill is passed by without a second glance. Both sites were used as locations for defensive castles (originally called York Castle and Old Baile) in an attempt to subdue the northern rebellions in the 11th century. But as time went on and the wear and tear of wars demanded necessary reconstructions, York Castle was rebuilt into Clifford's Tower and Old Baile was left to become a small forgotten hill.

The wooden castle of Old Baile that once stood on the man-made pile of earth that is now called Baile Hill was built in reaction to a rebellion against William the Conqueror. The King decided to subjugate Northumbria through a brutal military campaign that was dubbed the 'Harrying of the North'. As part of this, it was thought that more defences were needed to protect the king's authority: this new timber fortification was designed to mimic York Castle, which had been built on the other side of the river the previous year. It followed the motte-and-bailey layout (the motte is the big hill and the bailey is the enclosed courtyard below) – a tried and tested model of medieval military defence that can be seen all over Europe. Control of the fortress then passed to the Archbishop of York, with the stipulation that the city would come to the aid of the Old Baile if necessary, but the wooden castle soon became neglected, and the bailey was used only as a place for archery practice or cattle grazing.

NEARBY

Bitchdaughter Tower (28)

If you walk along the York wall trail path, you will soon find an odd circular room built into the corner of the wall. Looking almost like a medieval bunker, this was once the King's prison. The unusual name has evolved from the French *Biche dortoir* – loosely translated as 'wild animal dormitory'. Although the location of the gaol meant it was exposed to the worst of the elements, it wasn't all bad: it once even had an in-built fireplace and chimney.

Game (29)

Even further along the wall is another unusual quirk. A chess board has been carved into one of the stone paving slabs, thought to have been taken from the debtor's prison where inmates would have played in the yard. The board is still clear, so feel free to play a game on it, although other wall walkers won't thank you, and you'd have to bring your own pieces …

HENRY RICHARDSON'S MEMORIAL

A horse trough to honour the founder of York's RSPCA

Bishopsgate Street, YO23 1WH

A horse trough on the side of a road might not be the most prestigious of memorials, but the one on Bishopsgate Street is rather appropriate. Dedicated to Henry Richardson, a beloved local animal activist and businessman, it resides in the area that once formed part of the Cherry Hill Estate where he spent most of his working life as a manure manufacturer and agricultural merchant. Unfortunately, the trough, which was erected in 1905, has the incorrect date of death carved into it. Richardson died in 1893 rather than 1895 which generously gives him two more years than he actually had. The memorial is heartfelt all the same.

The Richardson family had lived in the Bishopsgate area for generations – Henry inherited the Cherry Hill Agricultural Business from his father and began to expand the firm into fertiliser production, although he soon left the active business-running to his partner

Around this time, he married Maria Heath, who was also well known for her activism and philanthropy.

Richardson was, by all accounts, a thoroughly good sort of man. Sitting on the board of multiple charitable organisations, speaking out for women's rights and volunteering at York's soup kitchens, he is most well known for co-founding the York branch of the Royal Society for the Protection of Cruelty to Animals (RSPCA) which started off life in a small brick building in St George's Field.

The choice of the horse trough as a memorial would have been due to the initial focus of the RSPCA on protection for working animals. It gives an indication as to how widespread horsepower (literally) was at the time. Although the trough is now used as a flower bed, it would have previously been crucial for watering the city's working horses, who were still the most reliable form of transport in the city when the trough was erected in 1905.

> The Christian proverb carved into the back commemorates Richardson's contribution to animal welfare, and epitomises his belief that 'a righteous man regardeth the life of his beast'.

THE NUNNERY WALL

Scandalous nuns

Clementhorpe, YO23 1AN

Naughty nuns always make for a good story, which is why it is surprising that the last remaining piece of the notorious Clementhorpe Nunnery barely features in any popular guides of the city. Although crumbling, the stone wall that once formed part of the nunnery can still be found on the quiet crossroads of Clementhorpe and Cherry Street, standing strangely detached from anything around it.

The nunnery of St Clements was set up in the 12th century as the first monastic institution created for women in the North of England. The sisters soon demonstrated their tenacity following a decision by the Archbishop of York which shifted power over the nunnery from the local priory of St Clements to the Abbey of Godstow, basically removing the nunnery's institutional independence. The sisters appealed to the Catholic authorities and the prioress was even said to have gone to Rome in person to set their case before the pope. Despite the Archbishop's attempt to excommunicate the nuns, the pope supported their claim, and they regained their position under St Clements.

The first public scandal at the nunnery concerned a young woman called Cecily who ran off with a local man, rejecting her religious responsibilities and living unmarried with her lover for three years. Later, Sister Isobel Studley was found guilty of *super laps carnis* (sins of the flesh) and apostasy (abandonment of religious belief). She was sent to another nunnery to serve her punishment and was only allowed back to Clementhorpe after she had sworn before God never to be blasphemous and quarrelsome ever again.

A greater scandal involved the infamous Joan Saxton, who not only escaped the nunnery, but went so far as to fake her own death and arrange a funeral for a dummy-body to ensure she would not be tracked down. Eventually she was found and returned to York, but Joan's story was so fantastical that it became the inspiration for Candace Robb's historic novel *The Nun's Tale*. However, it was not only the women of the priory who were involved in the Clementhorpe impropriety. A priest called John was accused of spiritual incest with a nun at Clementhorpe – spiritual incest being relations between a 'brother and sister' in the service of Christ.

The nunnery was dissolved in the 16th century, and progressively the structure was knocked down, leaving only one wall to remember York's only medieval nunnery and the free-spirited sisters of St Clements.

THE INSCRIPTION OF THE WATERFRONT HOUSE BAKERY

The co-operation of bread

Waterfront House, Clementhorpe, YO23 1PL

In the corner of the wall of Waterfront House, now apartments overlooking the River Ouse, there is a very discreet inscription detailing the original purpose of the building. Until the late 1960s this apartment block was a bread factory. The purpose was to produce large quantities of baked bread to sell at local stores – it was part of York's first venture into the co-operative business which had taken the North of England by storm in the 19th century.

The basic premise of the York Co-operative (also called the York Equitable Society) was that a community of traders would come together at the warehouse on Clementhorpe to provide the towns with wholesale produce. This produce would then go to the co-op branches. Regular people could buy membership of the co-operative, and when they purchased their groceries at the co-op branches, they would receive dividends for doing so, as well as having a voice in the running of the business. It was supposed to create the highest form of community spirit and democratic business.

Although the York Co-operative had only started in the mid-1800s, 50 years later it had expanded so much that the company needed a central location to help co-ordinate the different activities it was involved in. The bakery was a welcome addition to the general co-operative complex which by 1903, when the bakery was built, already had a bacon factory, coal wharf, office, oat crusher and stables on site. By the time it closed, the bakery was shifting around 18,000 loaves of bread each week. At its peak the York Co-operative numbered 10,000 members.

Not only concerned with food and groceries, the society also ran an Educational Committee which organised lectures and paid for school classes for members' families. The society eventually became a political party, with the man named in the inscription on the wall, W. H. Shaw, being the first member of York City Council who won as a Co-operative Society candidate. Your local co-op is a descendant of this idea.

FLOOD BOARD

(33)

How high does it go?

Tower Street, YO1 9SA

When York floods, it really floods. Half-submerged pubs and underwater paths have unfortunately been a regular sight on the banks between the Ouse and Skeldergate bridges. To see the levels that the water has reached over the years, there is a useful but little-known flood measurement board concealed in the bushes at the entrance to Tower Gardens that notes the height of the more destructive floods, tracking all the way back to 1638. The highest level on the board was reached in 2000, when the River Ouse rose 5.5 metres above its normal level.

NEARBY
Fossgate Barrier
Blue Bridge Lane, YO10 4AX

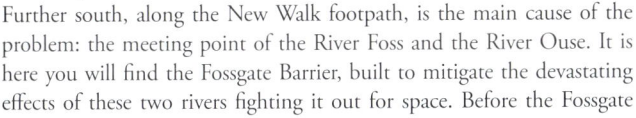

Further south, along the New Walk footpath, is the main cause of the problem: the meeting point of the River Foss and the River Ouse. It is here you will find the Fossgate Barrier, built to mitigate the devastating effects of these two rivers fighting it out for space. Before the Fossgate Barrier was built, whenever the water level rose in both these rivers, the Foss found it harder to flow into the Ouse. With nowhere to go, the water blocked up, rose further and the traffic jam of water led to widespread flooding, usually overflowing right back to the city centre. A particularly destructive flood in the late 1970s motivated the building of the barrier. The systems can control the movement of the river and pass any excess water from the Foss into the Ouse via an outflow pump, preventing the Foss from flooding further upstream.

A long line of 'blue bridges'

The brightly-coloured bridge overlooking the Fossgate Barrier has been here since 1929, but it is only the most recent in a long line of 'blue bridges' providing a crossing over the Foss. The first one was built in the 1730s – a little wooden drawbridge painted blue. This bridge gave way to stone, then to wood and then to iron. After the Crimean War, the bridge also had two intimidating cannons stationed at either end, but these were melted down during the Second World War to help with the war effort.

PUBLIC VEGETABLE BED

'If there's food you see, it's yours for free!'

Outside the entrance to the Barbican Centre, Paragon St, YO10 4AH
edibleyork.org.uk

The middle of a city seems like an unlikely place to find people foraging for wild food to eat. The most you might expect to see is the occasional walker picking a few blackberries to make a home-made apple and blackberry crumble. But in recent years, foraging has become popular both as a hobby and as an attempt to be more sustainable. The Public Veg Bed, an initiative designed by the horticultural charity Edible York, has created foraging for the modern city. Edible York own a number of community vegetable patches that offer free food to anyone walking past: according to Edible York's website, 'if there's food you see, it's yours for free!'

The primary purpose of the bed is to feed the people of York and foster a sense of community participation. The campaign began in 2010 with the first Veg Bed being planted by volunteers outside the York Barbican Centre. Although the rows of plants look quite out of place in front of the concrete building, they act as a reminder of the importance of healthy living and sustainable practice within urban life.

The upkeep of the miniature allotment falls to a team of locals who call themselves FOBBY (Friends of Barbican Bed Edible York). They change the edible plant menu every year, growing everything from sweet peas to herbs, and currents to kale – occasionally they give out free seed packets alongside the vegetables for people to grow at home.

Edible York aims to educate and engage people of all ages in the practice of gardening and horticulture, with the ultimate ambition being that every single person in York will soon grow, cook and eat their own food.

As well as the Public Veg Beds, the charity has a number of initiatives to turn this idea into a reality. The 'Patchwork Orchard' plants edible fruit trees around the city, creating a network of metropolitan orchards that has so far grown over 300 new trees. Another project, 'Abundance', is a harvesting exercise which aims to reduce waste by identifying wild fruit trees around the city whose fruit can be donated to food charities. The organisation is always looking for new initiatives to help make York a horticultural paradise, so be on the lookout for new gardening freebies popping up around the city.

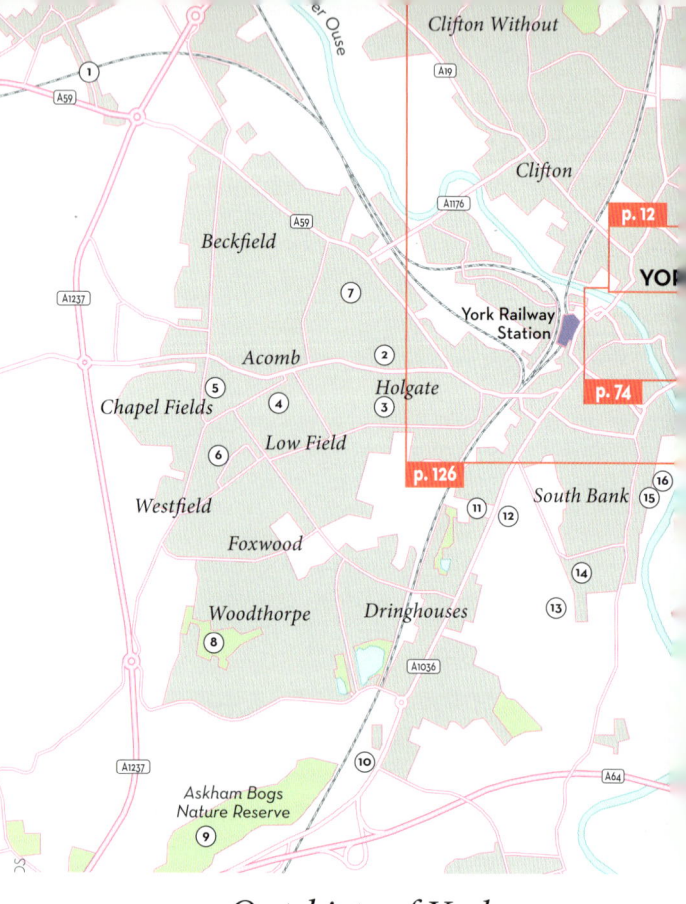

Outskirts of York

①	POPPLETON RAILWAY NURSERY	178
②	THE COLD WAR BUNKER	180
③	HOLGATE WINDMILL	182
④	THE NOSE OF QUEEN VICTORIA'S STATUE	184
⑤	WHITE ROW	186
⑥	ST AIDAN'S CHURCH	187
⑦	BACHELOR HILL	188
⑧	THE SEVERUS WATER TOWER	189
⑨	ACOMB WOOD AND MEADOW LOCAL NATURE RESERVE	190
⑩	ASKHAM BOG	192
⑪	THE SOLAR SYSTEM CYCLE PATH	194
⑫	THE PLAGUE STONE	196
⑬	THE TYBURN STONE	198
⑭	A SUNSET WALK AT YORK RACECOURSE	200

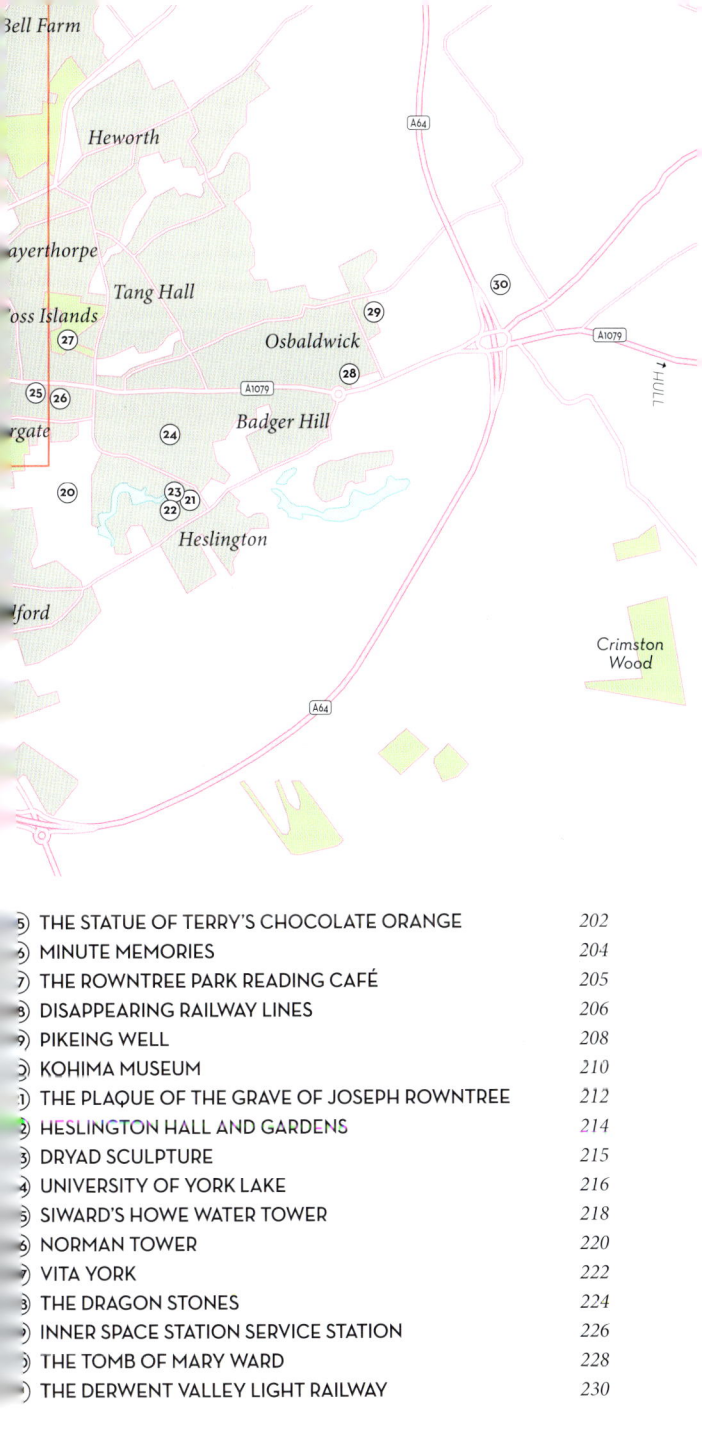

15	THE STATUE OF TERRY'S CHOCOLATE ORANGE	202
16	MINUTE MEMORIES	204
17	THE ROWNTREE PARK READING CAFÉ	205
18	DISAPPEARING RAILWAY LINES	206
19	PIKEING WELL	208
20	KOHIMA MUSEUM	210
21	THE PLAQUE OF THE GRAVE OF JOSEPH ROWNTREE	212
22	HESLINGTON HALL AND GARDENS	214
23	DRYAD SCULPTURE	215
24	UNIVERSITY OF YORK LAKE	216
25	SIWARD'S HOWE WATER TOWER	218
26	NORMAN TOWER	220
27	VITA YORK	222
28	THE DRAGON STONES	224
29	INNER SPACE STATION SERVICE STATION	226
30	THE TOMB OF MARY WARD	228
31	THE DERWENT VALLEY LIGHT RAILWAY	230

POPPLETON RAILWAY NURSERY

Britain's last railway nursery

Poppleton Station, Station Road, Upper Poppleton, YO26 6PZ
poppletonrailwaynursery.co.uk
See website for opening hours

Poppleton's tiny train station is the next stop along the Northern Railway Line from York Station. It has a charming village atmosphere, made all the more wholesome by the Poppleton Railway Nursery, now the last of its kind left in Britain.

A railway nursery is a cross between an allotment and a garden centre but based within a train station. They were originally used to grow vegetables for railway employees, in an attempt by the companies to keep their workers healthy and well-fed.

Most railway nurseries started up during the Second World War, when the need for sustainable vegetable growing arose alongside the introduction of food rationing. Poppleton Railway Station, like many others at the time, used the land next to its train track to create an allotment to feed employees and supply food to the nearby Railway Hotels.

Once the war was over, Poppleton Nursery became focused on growing trees and shrubs. These were then used to contribute natural resources to the post-war construction sites which were spread across the country after the devastating impact of air raids. Soon, the horticultural focus expanded and the nursery began to grow flowers and create hanging baskets to make the stations look prettier for the increasing number of railway users.

Poppleton Railway Nursery is now leased to the community on a peppercorn rent. Its volunteers grow all sorts of horticultural goodies which are then sold to the public, given to the railway workers or distributed around the area to other stations. The grounds themselves stood empty and neglected for many years, but were brought back to life in 2009 thanks to the efforts of a few local railway enthusiasts: the nursery is now full of old railway antiques to admire alongside the flowers, and the site itself is a wonderfully confused mismatch of railway buildings and greenhouses, linked by a winding railway track which passes around the site. It is also used by community groups who employ horticultural therapy to improve individual well-being and confidence. It now sells a vast array of plants, flowers and vegetables. The profits all go towards the long-lasting preservation of the nursery.

THE COLD WAR BUNKER

York's plan in case of nuclear attack

Monument Close, Holgate, YO24 4HT
english-heritage.org.uk/visit/places/york-cold-war-bunker
Check website for opening hours and prices

York's stone walls are famous for protecting the city in medieval times, but not many know that the city also has the infrastructure to deal with a much more modern threat: a nuclear attack. In 1961, a bunker was built on the outskirts of the city to detect atomic activity and nuclear fallout. It was one of many built by the government in the 1960s; however, while others were sold off or deteriorated after the Soviet Union fell in 1991, York's bunker, being located on government land, was protected. Eventually English Heritage bought the site for the public. Volunteers now provide tours of the bunker a few times a week, giving visitors the chance to explore the underground world of the Cold War.

The bunker was built in the middle of a residential area as a deliberate way for the government to demonstrate that they were protecting citizens from existential nuclear threats. Decorated with a sign that reads 'Vigilant State', the bunker does have a certain Orwellian atmosphere, particularly in the subterranean operations room. This is the central hub, designed to monitor nuclear attack and fallout. What was state-of-the-art technology is placed around the room, still laid out as it was for the training exercises that took place in the 30 years between the 1960s and the 1990s.

A triangulation table in the corner of the ops room shows a map of Yorkshire and the other monitoring posts based around the county. Each post had a 'fixed survey meter' – a piece of tech that could measure radiation levels. Telephonists would call into the stations, track radiation levels, pass the information to the observers working on the maps, and together build a county-wide picture of energy fallout. The bunker also contains fascinating 1960s equipment, like the light-sensitive 'ground zero indicator' to pinpoint the location, diameter and height of an explosion, or the 'bomb power indicator' to measure the size of the explosion.

When the bunker was erected, the government sent out a call for local volunteers who would undergo training exercises every month to prepare them for monitoring fallout in case of an attack. If the worst were to happen, the first 60 observers to get to the bunker would be let in and put in charge of the reconnaissance. The bunker held everything they needed to live for 30 days in a post-apocalyptic world – a recirculating air conditioning unit, an emergency water tank and supplies, but after that they would be on their own. Luckily, the training they undertook was never necessary, and the bunker remains a ghost of a war that never happened.

HOLGATE WINDMILL

The last one turning

Windmill Rise, YO26 4TX
holgatewindmill.org
On visitor days, information on website
The shop is open every Saturday 10am–noon

York was once home to as many as 20 windmills and four watermills, all using the power of nature to grind grain into flour. But with the coming of the industrial revolution, steam began to replace wind and water as the key energy source, and these icons of rural production began to disappear. Holgate Windmill is now the only working mill that remains in the city.

It has stood here since 1770 when it was built to support George Waud's family-run flour business. If you approach the windmill from the narrow alleyway that leads up from Acomb Road, you will be following the original horse and cart path which connected the mill to its local suppliers. The surrounding area was redeveloped for housing in the 1960s, so no other reminder of the original rural setting remains. The mill now sits on one of the housing estate's roundabouts, probably the most unusual location for an idyllic rural windmill that can be found anywhere in the country.

Considering its age, Holgate Windmill is looking well. Although the mill became inactive in the 1930s, the formation of the Holgate Windmill Preservation Society in 2001 successfully brought the retired windmill back to life. This 11-year project was run by local volunteers and included everything from a complete interior renovation to the construction of five new sails.

This number of sails makes Holgate Windmill even more unusual. Although more sails equal more power, most windmills have only four, so that if one sail breaks, then the one opposite can be removed, and the balance of the remaining two on each side allows the turbine to keep spinning. This cannot be done with a five-sail design, but despite this disadvantage, the restoration team decided to stick to the original design, making Holgate the oldest five-sail windmill in England.

Today the mill continues to be run by volunteers who provide stoneground wheat and spelt flour to the community, made in the traditional way (with a little help from electricity).

'Best British Roundabout'

Those familiar with the Roundabout Appreciation Society may recognise the roundabout underneath Holgate Windmill as the previous winner of the 'Best British Roundabout' award, and the poster child of the society's annual calendar. It was described by the society's president as 'totally unique' and 'a work of art', and it is the only roundabout in the world to have a working windmill on top of it.

THE NOSE OF QUEEN VICTORIA'S STATUE

④

A wandering statue

West Bank Park
5 Hill Street, Acomb, YO24 4JB
Daily 7.30am–9pm

Queen Vic is not looking too sparkly anymore. Found in a corner of West Bank Park, she is now stuck in between bushes and barely noticeable. Although she is made from Carrara marble, which would have been a dazzling white when it was first sculpted, over the years the forces of nature have worn away the shine of her marble and given her a strong yellow tinge: as the artist George Milburn stressed, the sculpture was never meant to be outside.

Vandals and statue-haters have also chopped off her nose (now replaced with a shiny new one) and taken her sceptre. Queen Victoria will always carry herself with dignity, but for a statue that was unveiled by a member of the Royal Family and designed to stand in the great Municipal Hall of York, it is quite a fall from grace.

The idea of a commemorative statue for the then recently deceased Queen Victoria was surrounded by controversy from the beginning. Although everyone in government in the early 1900s agreed that the city must have a citizen's memorial to Her Majesty, opinion on what type of memorial it should be fell into two different political camps. The Conservatives wanted a true-to-life statue which would stand in their Guildhall, but the Liberals wanted a memorial park to be named Victoria Park. The Conservative majority got their way, and after a long battle, received enough public donations to begin the design competition for the new statue.

The winner of the competition, who was a local sculptor, was also the topic of a few heated debates around geographical nepotism – as it was thought that anyone from outside York had not seriously been considered for the prize. Whether this was true or not, it certainly contributed to the increasing sense of grudge against the statue.

Being built larger than life – the statue measures 1.75 metres whereas the real Queen Victoria was barely 1.5 metres – meant that the effigy began to get in the way once it had found its home in the Guildhall. The constant reminder of the Conservatives' political bulldozering also grated on the increasingly Liberal local government, and the statue was eventually moved to the Exhibition Buildings (now York Art Gallery) in 1912. The effigy's awkward size returned as an issue after the curators decided the room was needed for a new exhibition. She was sentenced to exile, banished to the outskirts of the city and placed in West Bank Park.

WHITE ROW

⑤

Little white houses

48 Front Street, Acomb, YO24 3BX

The Acomb area of York is rarely explored. It does not have many of the typical medieval buildings or obvious tourist attractions that might persuade people to venture this far out from the centre, but the beauty of Acomb lies in the few unique architectural gems that are scattered among its village houses. White Row is one such example.

The long row of tiny white terraced cottages, each of which looks almost too small to be a separate house, stands apart from the general look of the town in both colour and design. They were built in the 17th century as 'five little houses', at a time when the township was primarily a rural farming area.

After the First World War, York City Council wanted to expand their jurisdiction in order to set up affordable housing outside the city. Acomb was identified as an ideal location for these developments: by 1937 it had become part of the boundaries of York, but in the midst of the demolition of the old and construction of the new, White Row stayed where it was.

Over the years, White Row has been used as both living and working spaces. It has been a blacksmith's, a base for local businesses and a retirement village, but the long row of tiny houses and traditional arches has always stayed the same, adding something bright and interesting to the landscape of the town.

NEARBY

St Aidan's Church (6)

Ridgeway, Acomb, YO26 5DA

An icon of 1960s ecclesiastical architecture, the central spire and sloping roof that came from the creative minds of the Ferrey & Mennim design firm make St Aidan's look more like a radio studio complete with satellite than a place of worship. St Aidan's was built in 1968 as a 'daughter church' to support the growing parish of St Stephen's, which is Acomb's historic church on the other side of Acomb Green.

BACHELOR HILL

Views for miles

Askham Lane and Tennent Road, YO24 3HD

Surrounded on all sides by private homes and main roads, Bachelor Hill is a tricky spot to find. Accessed through two tiny entrances, one next to 71A Askham Lane, the other between 84 and 86 Tennent Road, the space initially looks like a deserted field with a small knoll and an empty sandpit. However, once you climb over the sandpit, up he knoll, and reach the family of trees that stand at the top of Bachelor Hill, you will know why it is worth discovering. From this point you can see panoramic views for miles, all the way from the sails of Holgate Windmill to the towers of York Minster.

Bachelor Hill is the highest point in Acomb, reaching about 30 metres above sea level, which is why it offers such breathtaking scenes of the city and the surrounding countryside. Being so cut off from main roads and other walking routes, the field is usually empty. This is good news for the local wildlife: the various breeds of butterflies that live around the sand dunes have space to play, and the field is home to many different species of wildflowers, including hare's-foot clover, pink restharrow and parsley-piert.

NEARBY

The Severus Water Tower (8)

Lindsey Ave, Holgate, YO26 4RR

From the top of Bachelor Hill you can also make out the distinctive outline of the Severus Water Tower. Named after Septimus Severus, a Roman Emperor who apparently died and was burned on a funeral pyre in Acomb, the water tower was used as part of the Acomb Water Treatment Works, until it was closed down following a dramatic incident involving burst mains. Although technology has moved on from when the Severus was constructed 80 years ago, the tower has yet to be demolished and has remained unused but stubbornly present within York's landscape for over a decade.

ACOMB WOOD AND MEADOW LOCAL NATURE RESERVE

York's last remaining wood and natural meadow

Acomb Wood Drive, Woodthorpe, YO24 3XN

York has a knack of fitting as many things as possible into one place, but sandwiching seven acres of woodland forest in between a tight array of housing estates is one of its best magic tricks. Acomb Wood does not even appear on Google Maps, which shows just how hidden it is. You can find the forest by googling Acomb Wood Drive and searching for the footpath next to the Tesco Express carpark. Alternatively, go to the end of Girvan Close or Skiddaw Road where there will be a small entrance that leads into the wood. At each of the approaches, a plaque gives information about the nature reserve and how it came to be.

An eclectic mix of trees grow in Acomb Wood, but the oak, birch, pine, holly and hazel are the most common. The canopy is also home to the tawny owl, the woodpecker and the treecreeper, not to mention the hundreds of small mammals and invertebrates living in the hedgerows. The meadow to the north of the wood is even more ecologically important: it is the last preserved example of a natural meadow in the city. Although York has one of the lowest levels of woodland cover in England (about 3%, which is low even for a city), it is thought that this whole area was once completely covered in forest.

The name Acomb comes from the Old English word *acum*, meaning 'at the oaks'. And yet, Acomb Wood is now one of only two ancient forests in all of York. It is at least three times smaller than it was in medieval times, due to years upon years of development encroaching on the natural habitats that had survived here for generations. It was only in 2007 when activists stepped in and fought to protect the area as a local nature reserve that this ended. The section of the wood that lies on the east side of Acomb Wood Drive is owned by York City Council and watched over by the Friends of Acomb Wood, who host regular meetings, clean-up sessions and community programmes. The west side is now protected by the Woodland Trust.

ASKHAM BOG

One of the most biodiverse wildlife habitats in the North of England

Askham Bryan, YO23 3QX
ywt.org.uk/nature-reserves/askham-bog-nature-reserve
Bus 3 park and ride to Askham Bar

Askham Bog's excuse for being so wet and soggy is that it was born in the Ice Age. Fifteen-thousand years ago, when glaciers were slowly moving over this ground, the motion of the dense slabs of ice created a dip in the earth which filled with melted glacial water and eventually became sodden with thousands of years' worth of rain, snow and hail. Askham Bog is fundamentally just a very wet bowl (although the website refers to it as an ancient lake), and because of its unusual natural history, the nature reserve has become one of the most biodiverse wildlife habitats in the North of England.

The canopy of trees, the towering reeds and the assorted animal inhabitants make it the perfect place to escape from the city, especially as it is quiet and empty for most of the year. You can bring your wellies and dive straight into the ditches or take the elevated wooden walkway that carves out a path through the bog and offers an occasional information plaque describing the various flora and fauna to look out for.

The land was only officially bought for conservation in 1946 by the confectionery businessmen Sir Frances Terry and Arnold Rowntree. It was a joint philanthropic venture – the chocolate team gifted the area to the newly created York Naturalists Trust for safekeeping. Preservation of the bog was the first purpose of the society and conservationists around the country still see the area as crucial to the advancement of knowledge of natural species. Water control is a key issue, and the Naturalists Trust have been working hard to minimise the level of water loss and ensure the bog does not dry up: it has built dams, removed shrubs and created a pond. But natural destruction is not the only threat. Locals and activists have had to fight hard to conserve the bog from development schemes. Even Sir David Attenborough once felt compelled to step into the debate and publicly denounce potential housing plans on the area – an impressive celebrity endorsement for a little marsh just outside the city.

THE SOLAR SYSTEM CYCLE PATH ⑪

Cycling faster than the speed of light

Cycle path just off Sim Balk Lane, YO23 2UB

As you leave York on the bicycle track going in the direction of Selby, for every 100 metres you travel you will have covered 57 million kilometres in space: the 6.4-mile route that once formed part of the East Coast railway line has been transformed into an intergalactic journey through our solar system, at a scale of 575,872,239 to 1.

Models of all the planets are found along the cycle path (Pluto makes an appearance, as well as a couple of spacecraft) and each sculpture gives a little description of the planet's characteristics and discovery. The cycle path, as a whole, is therefore a beautiful and instructive way to understand better the scale and distances of the solar system.

The space-path was officially opened in 1999 after six months of planet-building. The bases of the models are made from old sewer pipes filled with concrete and most of the stainless-steel planets went through an abrasive technique of shot blasting before being attached to their bases.

The only exception to this method is the Sun, whose enormous model was made from two halves of a fibreglass sphere, moulded together and attached to a steel frame, which then had ten tonnes of concrete added inside to ensure the whole thing would not blow over. It is naturally the first model to appear on the route – it hangs in the middle of a group of trees, almost levitating out of the bushes.

Aside from the planets, there are also two man-made space objects to be found: the Cassini spacecraft and the Voyager 1 space probe. The real Cassini spacecraft, named after the 17th-century Italian-French astronomer Giovanni Cassini, was launched in 1997 by a partnership of international space organisations in an unprecedented attempt to find out all there is to know about Saturn and its moons. It spent almost 20 years in outer space exploring Saturn's atmosphere, taking incredible pictures and samples of unexplored regions of the ringed planet, before the mission ended in 2017. York's Cassini sculpture was created to celebrate the 10th anniversary of the mission and can be found near the Saturn model.

Voyager 1 was also record-breaking in its achievements. It was launched in 1977 and is continuing on its journey further and further into outer space. In 2012, it became the first man-made object to enter the region between the stars, the interstellar atmosphere. In York it stays right where it is, at the last point of the trail, signalling the end of our solar system.

THE PLAGUE STONE

Self-isolation delivery service

Little Hob Moor, Tadcaster Road, YO24 1ET

Behind the entrance to Little Hob Moor fields are two stones standing side by side. The smaller of the two acted as a money deposit and was used after a particularly severe bout of the bubonic plague (also known as the Black Death) hit York in the 17th century.

Often, when someone who lived in York was very contagiously ill, it was considered safer to banish them entirely from the city centre rather than have them remain inside and risk infecting others. The banished sick would place money in the stone, fill it with vinegar to ensure the coins were not contaminated, and healthy city folk would leave parcels of food by the stone in return.

The bubonic plague killed one third of York's population during the 17th century.

Alongside the stone, there would have been wooden huts where the sick were taken to live until they recovered (or didn't).

> The taller of the two stones is a lot older and has nothing to do with plagues. It has been there since the 1300s and commemorates the De Ros family who donated the surrounding land to the poor so they could have land on which to farm. The stone had a figure of a knight carved into it, but only the bottom of his shield can now be seen. Before it became weather-worn there was a rhyming inscription on the stone that read 'this image long Hob's name has bore / who was a knight in time of yore / and gave this common to ye poor'.

More plague stones in York

Hob Moor's stone was not the only plague stone used to feed the quarantined sick – there were actually three more placed around the outskirts of the city, and another one can still be seen on Burton Stone Lane, at the front of Burton Stone Inn.

Ridge and furrow

If you take a stroll through Hob Moor you will notice the ground beneath you is a little bumpy. This is because of long lines of narrow ridge and furrow – an adapted agricultural technique of horse ploughing which was used extensively on this ground during the Napoleonic wars. A combination of poor harvest and the demands of war led to massive economic uncertainty – the moor was rented out to the York Corporation to produce a supply of grain to keep the city fed. They created the lines of ridge and furrow which can still be felt over 200 years later.

THE TYBURN STONE
The drop

286 Tadcaster Road, YO24 1ET

The Tyburn, named after the more famous London Tyburn execution stand, was a three-post wooden construction used in York as an execution platform until the early 19th century. Despite hosting its last execution 200 years ago, the Tyburn area still remains a very sombre part of York. The view over the vast Knavesmire fields creates a feeling of isolation, and the canopy of trees seems to darken the mood as well as the light. The singular stone placed in the middle of the ground acts as a simple, but effectively grim, reminder that men and women were executed on this very spot for over 400 years.

Yet, despite the sense of gloom that is cast over the place now, back in the 14th century attending an execution would have been considered one of the best public activities of the year. The whole town would make the journey to Tyburn to watch the execution of petty thieves and religious dissenters. It was a form of entertainment that was enthusiastically encouraged by the city authorities, who needed public support in order to continue with their capital punishment sentences.

A soldier called Edward Hewlson was the first person to test out the newly built 'three-legged mare' in 1379, having been convicted of rape. After him followed a whole host of gallows victims, including the infamous highwayman Dick Turpin (see page 100), until the last person was executed on the Tyburn in 1801.

To add to their punishment, all the prisoners also had to make the mile-long journey from the centre of the city with their coffin and the general public alongside them. One of the main reasons that the Tyburn was taken down was due to this distance – the long journey was starting to become unpopular with the locals, probably a mixture of morality and laziness, and with diminishing public support, capital punishment sentences were becoming infrequent. The authorities also wanted to reduce the huge crowds of people gathering around the exits of the city on execution days. A spot near the Judge's Court (called the York Assizes) was used instead as it was right next to Clifford's Tower, and was therefore a much more convenient location for a day out to the gallows.

The name Tyburn means 'place of elms'. In old English: elm was used to construct the platform and it also had a long symbolic relationship with coffin-makers.

A SUNSET WALK AT YORK RACECOURSE

One of the best walking spots in the city

Racecourse Road, Knavesmire Road, YO23 1EX
Bus 197 (shuttle bus) from York Railway Station runs daily 11am–1pm
Grasslands and the racetrack on Knavesmire fields are open all day

With all the crowds that usually flock to York Racecourse, it is hard to get a proper view of the incredible buildings and beautiful location that support the festivities. But, little known to visitors and locals alike, the grasslands and even the racetrack on Knavesmire fields are open all day, and if you get there after hours – especially around sunset, or early in the morning – you will often find that you have the entire racecourse to yourself. Peaceful and quite stunning, it is possibly one of the best walking spots in the city, and it gives you a chance to really appreciate the monumental achievement that is York Racecourse.

A racecourse first appeared on Knavesmire fields in 1730, but for 20 years it was just a horseshoe-shaped track; it only became what we would describe as a modern racecourse when John Carr built the world's first grandstand overlooking the track, exclusively for the use of the wealthy patrons that had financed its construction. Many renovations have taken place over the years, including the addition of the new and impressive five-storey grandstand. Carr's original building has become the Guinness Bar.

The first female jockey

The track also hosted a race with the first female jockey. Alicia Thornton challenged her brother-in-law William Flint to a race in 1804 – she had previously beaten him in a less formal environment and the pair decided the re-match required a more prestigious setting. They both rode well, but halfway through the race Alicia's saddle became loose, her horse Vinagrillo fell lame and she was unable to finish. Incredibly over 100,000 people came to place bets and cheer them on, and despite the result, Alicia's impressive riding was the talk of the town. Her husband, Colonel Thornton, was considered decidedly eccentric for 'turning his lady into a racing jockey'.

THE STATUE OF TERRY'S CHOCOLATE ORANGE

An ode to the former chocolate factory

Clocktower Way, YO23 1PX

As a nod to the Chocolate Works' chocolatey past, the Malton Sherburn Foundry created a giant brass statue of a Terry's Chocolate Orange and tucked it away in one of the courtyards of York's new housing development. These luxury apartments and offices were once part of Terry's Art-Deco style chocolate factory estate. Nearby, is the old main factory. It is Grade II listed and so protected from significant alterations, which is why you can still wander around the site and get a sense of the huge international confectionery business that was once based there.

Built in 1926, the huge factory exemplified the transformation of Terry's Chocolate into a global company. The business had started as a partnership back in 1767 when it was a small shop selling crystalised fruit sweets. The sales increased and the store moved to the prime location of St Helen's Square in the centre of York – you can still see the 'Terry's' sign carved into the building there.

The apothecary Joseph Terry became the sole owner of the company in the early 19th century and the business went from strength to strength, passing down from father to son, until it required the space of a massive factory complex: Terry's Chocolate Works. It remained a confectionery factory until 2004 when the company was taken over by Kraft foods. Production moved overseas and the York site became private housing.

The famous Chocolate Orange was once an apple

A little-known fact about the famous Chocolate Orange is that it actually started life as an apple. Terry's 'Dessert Chocolate Apple' was created in 1926 as an after-meal apple-flavoured delicacy – it was only ten years later that the Orange first appeared. From the start it was clear that orange was a far more popular flavour, and in time the apple production stopped, allowing the iconic Terry's Chocolate Orange to hit the stage as a solo act. The Apple and the Orange were not the only adventures in chocolate flavours. Once Terry's had been taken over by Colgate-Palmolive in the late 1970s, they attempted a Chocolate Lemon, to work alongside their scented soaps. Needless to say, no one wanted to eat anything that reminded them of soap and the campaign was a resounding failure.

MINUTE MEMORIES

Recorded voices of York's past

Rowntree Park, Richardson Street, YO23 1JU

Installed at the Richardson Street entrance to Rowntree Park, stationed in a flowerbed behind a rail and almost completely camouflaged by tall plants, is a small metal object that looks like an oddly placed intercom. As the adjacent sign explains, this is the 'York Remembers Rowntree' memory post: with a simple turn of the dial you can listen to a collection of oral history recordings from eight locals whose lives were in some way influenced by York's famous chocolate family, the Rowntrees.

These interviews were part of a larger memory collection project which was led by the Rowntree foundation in 2013. It recorded the experiences of those who had benefited from the legacy of the Rowntree organisation, such as those who worked in the Rowntree factory, which at its peak employed 14,000 people in York. The interviews were based around themes such as leisure, work, entertainment and New Earswick: by the end of the project in 2015 the team had completed 40 valuable interviews.

One year after starting the project, the foundation chose a selection of highlights from the wide range of recordings and put them in a permanent audio-post for park visitors to hear. When the post was fitted, the Rowntree Reading Room Café also held an accompanying exhibition where participants donated objects of interest related to their experience of Rowntree.

NEARBY

The Rowntree Park Reading Café (17)
Rowntree Park Lodge, Richardson St, YO23 1JU

The Rowntree Park Reading Café can be found on the first floor of the Park Lodge, in the centre of the Joseph Rowntree Memorial Park. In one of the most ornamentally picturesque parts of the city, the café is a lovely place to spend an afternoon, and (continuing the Quaker tradition of improving the hearts and minds of the community) in 2012 the tearoom proclaimed itself the UK's first public library reading café. As libraries around the country faced difficulties with lower membership and reduced funding, York's library community decided to free themselves from the restrictions of the City Council and open a new library in a central location with an adapted purpose: instead of a library, it would be a reading café. The shelves are packed with literary options, and they are all available for anyone who wants to spend a quintessentially British afternoon with a good book and a cup of tea.

DISAPPEARING RAILWAY LINES

Vestige of the Royal Ordinance Corps depot

New Walk, YO10 4EF

Along the footpath next to the River Ouse, near the Millennium Bridge, is the ghost of an old railway track disappearing into a brick wall. It is the last vestige of the Royal Ordinance Corps depot which transported goods and equipment from 'powder boats' moored on the riverbank into the stores of Fulford Military Barracks. The small section of railway track is the only part of this local military station that can still be seen.

The Royal Ordinance Corps was the section of the British Army that had responsibility for the provisions and maintenance of military equipment. It was their job to support and supply the military barracks which used to stand in the area over the wall.

After the Corps was set up in York in 1890, they constructed a purpose-built wharf onto the river, and a mini railway to link the wharf and the barracks. The railway was used to transport the goods into and around the military complex.

The mini railway was moved by horses or men, rather than steam engine, because the risk of explosions would have been too high. The tracks were used until the 1950s when the barracks were moved to a different location. The building was converted into a civilian hospital and the unused tracks began to fade into the grass. The railway was rediscovered during the New Walk Millenium Project after the entire area was excavated, but because a new wall had since been put up, the railway tracks now mysteriously lead from nowhere to nowhere.

Shameless officers

The area around the Fulford Barracks was considered a very insalubrious part of town in the early part of the 19th century. 'Fallen women' were said to pick up clientele on the banks of the river, men would meet for dog fighting, and naked bathing was a continuous issue for the council. Some of the original houses on New Walk Terrace were said to have been built for the mistresses of the officers. It is now one of York's most desirable places to live.

PIKEING WELL

The power of water

New Walk, YO10 4BG

If you were suffering from some sort of ailment and looking to recover your health, Pikeing Well is probably the last place you would go. A dark pit inside an arched brick cave, the locked well on the bank of the River Ouse is not part of anyone's well-being weekend retreat plans nowadays. But it was once one of the highlights of Georgian York – a spot for upper-class recuperation and rejuvenation.

Pikeing Well featured as part of the 'New Walk', a fashionable 18th-century promenade along the River Ouse designed by the City Corporation as a leisure pursuit, or what they called 'innocent entertainment'. The fashion of strolling came over to England from Europe, and York was merely trying to keep up with the trend – by this time many towns around the country already had their own outdoor promenades for the gentry to meet, walk and gossip.

The New Walk was continually adapted to ensure it remained popular – in 1752 Pikeing Well was added, appealing to the contemporary health trend of drinking fresh spring water. To create a sense of privacy, John Carr was hired to design the 'grotto' over the well. This was his first project in York, and he went on to become one of England's most prestigious architects. The Corporation controlled access to the grotto, hired a ticket attendant to hold the key to the gate and charged a fee for the pleasure of drinking from inside the cave.

Many lords and ladies made the journey to indulge in the healing powers of Pikeing Well's spring water. Lady Middlethorpe was one notable York society visitor, having been advised that her son's rickets would be cured after a visit to the cave. Interestingly, Lady Middlethorpe was an enthusiastic follower of modern medicine and an early supporter of vaccination, so her belief in the medicinal power of spring water is somewhat surprising. The practice went on until 1929 when the Ministry of Health cut off the water supply – it had been discovered that the spring water actually drained through the extended York Cemetery, weaving between the buried bodies, and therefore was perhaps not as clean and pure as the visitors might expect.

KOHIMA MUSEUM ⑳

'When you go home tell them of us and say, for your tomorrow we gave our today'

Imphal Barracks
Fulford Road, YO10 4HD
01904 665806
kohimamuseum.co.uk
Thursday 9am–noon or at any time via prior appointment

At the very back of York's infantry barracks is a tiny museum dedicated exclusively to a single military event which helped turn the tide of World War II: the battle of Kohima, in North East India, in 1944. Being hidden away in a military complex, it is almost unknown to those who are not part of the direct history. Visitors will need to register at the barrack's reception before being escorted through the site to the museum.

This specialist museum has become a place of pilgrimage for the relatives of those who fought in the battle. It has the most extensive archive of Kohima-related objects in the world, including military medals, giant strategic maps and letters that were sent home from the soldiers. The reason why a battle fought halfway across the world is now memorialised at the back of a York barracks is because of the crucial role of the Yorkshire Regiments.

The York Infantry Barracks were built in the late 19th century as a living quarters for a localised unit called the West Yorkshire Regiment. During the Second World War these men were sent out to Kohima to hold the supply base there. In 1944, the Japanese invaded India and surrounded Kohima to prevent the soldiers from sending goods and equipment to the important strategic city of Imphal a few miles to the south. The subsequent battle was one of the bloodiest of the war, with brutal hand-to-hand combat leading to the death of over 11,000 soldiers on both sides. The fighting lasted for almost three months and the British managed to hold the area. Back home, the barracks were renamed Imphal Barracks in honour of those who fought.

A mysterious but moving story lies behind the acquisition of the Japanese helmet that is displayed in one of the cabinets. The helmet, peppered with bullet holes, was dropped off by a Japanese man who insisted that it needed to be preserved here – a strong reminder that brave men fought and died on both sides of the battle.

THE PLAQUE OF THE GRAVE OF JOSEPH ROWNTREE

Rowntree's concealed grave

The wall of The Retreat
Walmgate Stray, YO10 5NG

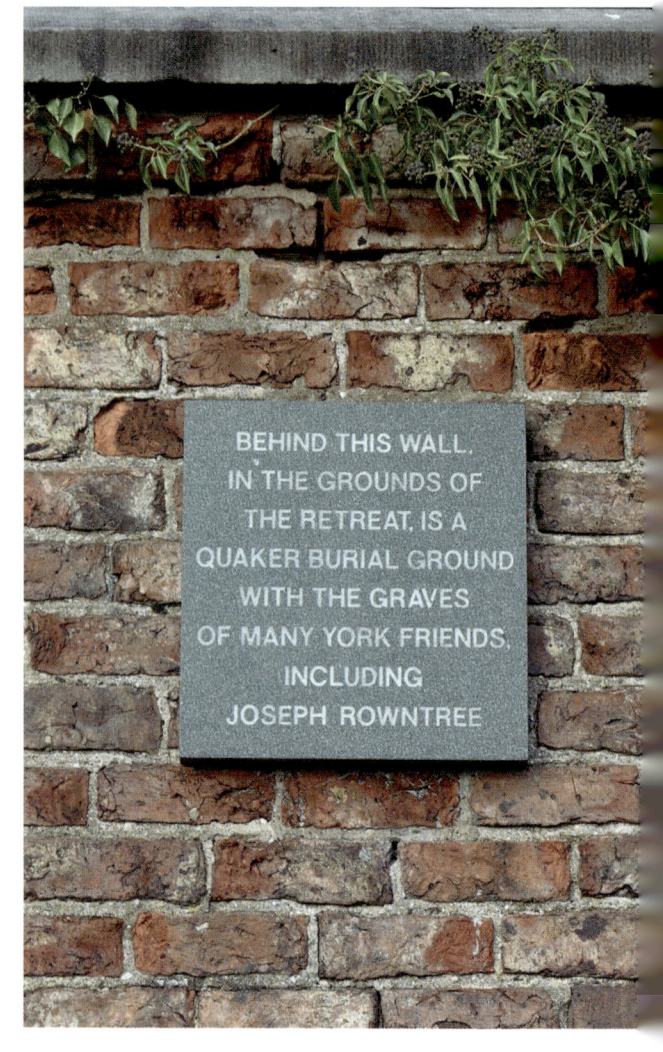

Joseph Rowntree's impact on York cannot be overstated. He employed thousands of people, supported the city's commercial industry and gave millions to philanthropic causes. For someone so renowned in the city's history, you would think his grave would be found somewhere central and prestigious, allowing locals and tourists alike to pay their respects. Instead, he is buried behind a high brick wall overlooking the remote fields of Walmgate Stray in the private grounds of an old psychiatric hospital – the grave is therefore inaccessible to the general public. The only indication that Rowntree is buried there is the small grey sign attached to the wall, far from the path, that reads 'Behind this wall, in the grounds of the retreat, is a Quaker burial ground with the graves of many York friends including Joseph Rowntree'.

The Retreat is a mental health clinic that has been treating patients in York for over 200 years. The building and the long winding wall surrounding it were built in the late 18th century by the Quaker William Tuke. It was designed to be a more ethical mental health facility than the horrendous psychiatric institutes common in that period, such as the York Lunatic Asylum (see page 148). Instead of practising cruelty (in an attempt to 'beat' the madness out of patients), the inmates at The Retreat were given private rooms, easy tasks to complete and psychiatric treatment according to moral Quaker principles. News of this innovative treatment spread across the world, with many people coming to The Retreat to see it for themselves.

The Quaker community remained strong in York and many famous names were buried in the grounds of the institute. Joseph Rowntree, among his many other activities, was governor of The Retreat for 40 years, and his family continued to take an active role in the hospital's community. Which is why, when he died in 1925, he was buried in the grounds and eventually joined by many members of his family.

HESLINGTON HALL AND GARDENS

A stunning area, usually deserted

University of York, Heslington, YO10 5DZ

Tucked away in the grounds of the University of York is Heslington Hall and its landscaped gardens. This stunning area is the oldest and most beautiful part of the campus, but because it is separated from student accommodation and lecture halls, it is usually deserted. You can walk around the grounds and admire the impressive medieval building or perfectly clipped giant trees, or find your way to the small tower which acts as the entrance to a secret walled garden and meditation room for students.

For most of its life, Heslington Hall was owned by local aristocrats. Things changed with the Second World War when the wealthy family who owned it – the Deramores – evacuated, leaving it to become the location for York RAF Bomber Command.

The RAF seemed to have had a good time at the old aristocratic manor: one of the Deramores's stuffed rhinoceroses was even known to join them for a few pints at the local pub.

The Deramores never came back for their house or their rhino: in the 1950s, the deserted Hall was purchased by the Joseph Rowntree Social Services Trust on the advice of its chairman, J.B. Morrell. He initially had great plans for an idyllic country space for the public, filled with maypoles and water mills, but eventually decided a university would be of more use. With the landscape gardens and the countryside atmosphere of Heslington, the area seems like a good balance between the two ideals of country space and academic institution. But when the grounds were first discussed as a potential location for a new university, Heslington Hall was not a good advertisement. The Hall was run-down and dilapidated, and many people thought that the idea of building a university here was completely unrealistic. It took a lot of convincing and a makeover for Heslington) to get the support needed before the University was able to open its doors in 1963.

NEARBY

Dryad sculpture (23)

University of York, Heslington, YO10 5DZ

Displayed in the gardens is a sculpture by one of York's most prestigious 20th-century artists. Awarded an honorary degree from the University in the 1970s, Austin Wright designed this dryad (tree nymph) while he was living in artistic isolation with his wife in an old barn only a few miles away. Influenced by the York landscape, the statue is one of Wright's only surviving outdoor pieces.

UNIVERSITY OF YORK LAKE

The largest man-made, plastic-bottomed lake in Europe

University of York, University Road, Heslington, YO10 5DD
Part of the Open University Campus

The lake which takes centre stage at York University Campus is a record holder: it is the largest man-made, plastic-bottomed lake in Europe.

The 15-acre lake is the central feature of the University's landscape design and was added to the campus for a few reasons. Symbolically, the designers thought having a water feature would foster a sense of community; practically, it created a drainage site for the flat land.

The marsh borders and surrounding fauna were designed to create biodiversity; however, it has now been almost completely taken over by wildfowl, who have successfully led the University into achieving another record: holding one of the highest 'duck densities' in the country.

The Central Hall is the University of York's flagship building. Nicknamed 'the spaceship' it hovers over the campus as a beacon of controversial modernism. The concrete half-octagonal building marked a new era of university design in post-war Britain but it has since been on countless shortlists for the prize of Britain's ugliest building. Designed by RMJM, one of the largest architectural firms in the world, the spaceship functions as an assembly hall used for lectures, ceremonies and exams, all held in the huge circular auditorium. On top of its academic uses, the Hall has also featured as a filming location, exhibition space and concert hall.

The biggest duck ever to have lived?

The plastic-bottomed lake was home to a resident that was described (incorrectly) online as 'the biggest duck ever to have lived'. Long Boi stood at 70cm tall and was a cross between a mallard and an Indian Runner duck. Although very large compared to the other mallards around him, Long Boi was about average size for an Indian Runner, but he shot to fame after students created an online profile for him that now has over 47,000 followers.

SIWARD'S HOWE WATER TOWER ㉕

An abandoned water tower masquerading as a medieval castle

Heslington Hill, YO10 5NL

Masked by trees at the top of Heslington Hill is an abandoned building that looks like a cross between a dystopian prison and a medieval castle. You used to be able to see the whole structure, but over the years a growing thicket of trees and shrubs has created a thick barrier around it. Now, unless you trek through the forest path, you can only see the tops of the towers poking out from the foliage as you cross University Road.

The water tower was built in the 1950s to address the increasing demand for water coming from the growing population of York. The building supplied the city with one million gallons of water, although the adjoining reservoir added another ten million gallons to the site. For some reason, the Fine Arts Commission insisted at the time that the water tower be designed in the shape of a castle. The architectural design is clearly based on an old Norman castle, and some of the antennae could even pass as turrets if you squint hard enough.

Eventually the water system was moved to a different location and for a while the tower was used as storage for the sets and costumes of the York Theatre Royal. It is now abandoned and merely stands as an odd type of homage to York's medieval past.

Siward's Howe burial ground

The 'Howe' in Siward's Howe comes from the Old Norse word *Hleaw*, which was the name for an Anglo-Saxon or Viking burial ground preserved for people of high social standing. A rare example of one of these burial grounds can be found along the footpath from University Road, next to the University Library. The old burial ground looks like a mound of earth, but the elevated hill was specifically chosen so that the bodies could retain their high social status throughout the afterlife, overlooking the city from above. Beneath the grass are the graves of the most prestigious members of the society of ancient York, and the area has been protected by Historic England due to it being one of only around 50 in the country.

NORMAN TOWER

A tower without a church

St Lawrence Church, Lawrence Street, YO10 3WP

The current church of St Lawrence is the largest parish church in York: it is well known and well attended. Lesser known is the old Norman tower that resides in its graveyard: this lonely looking column was part of the previous church of St Lawrence, before it was demolished and replaced. Now detached from its original structure, the 11th-century tower has an unusual ornamental wooden doorway at its base, and now has an air of mystery and fantasy about it, something more than just the remains of a fairly typical medieval building.

The first St Lawrence church was built in the Norman period at the request of the Archbishop of York. It consisted of a rectangular building, a small tower and a stone arch decorated with intricate carvings of flowers and mythical creatures. Although some of the carvings have been recently restored, such as Sagittarius shooting his bow, many others are over 900 years old and part of the original framing.

During the English Civil War, the Parliamentarians set up guns under the St Lawrence tower and bombarded the walls of the city. There was hand-to-hand combat in the grounds, and the church was partially destroyed. The parish continued to use St Lawrence until 1883, by which time the congregation had increased by so much that a larger building was required. Most of the original church of St Lawrence was demolished, leaving only the empty tower and the doorway leading nowhere.

Frances Allen has the prestigious accolade of having the most interestingly shaped grave in the whole of St Lawrence's sizeable churchyard. It is cylindrical with a rounded top, supposedly shaped like a medicine pot. Both Frances and her husband Dr Oswald Allen worked for the York Dispensary Charity in the 1800s and her memorial was intended to illustrate her connection to York's public healthcare.

The beautiful but heartbreaking Riggs memorial, designed in the style of an Ancient Greek tomb, commemorates the six Riggs children who tragically drowned in the Ouse River in the 1830s. The incident shocked the nation, and the memorial now stands not only as a reminder of the tragedy, but also in remembrance of all those who have died in the river ever since.

VITA YORK

㉗

The nun-to-student housing

Lawrence Street, YO10 3FT
Available to look round on request hello@vitastudent.com

With the increasing number of undergraduates heading to York's two universities, student accommodation has been cropping up everywhere, even in former convents.

Inside the swanky interior-designed buildings of Vita York are the last traces of the Monastery of Poor Clare Nuns. The fusion of old nunnery and new student living makes for a brilliant design, and although the reception area keeps the riff-raff out, you can still tour the grounds if you ask in advance.

The Poor Clare Nuns were part of the Catholic Order of St Clare, and in the late 1800s, the St Lawrence Convent was built as their home. There, they were completely self-sufficient: they grew their own food, fasted for long periods at a time and always remained inside the high brick walls. The orchard where they picked fruit is still growing today and the grass is cut into the shape of a cross as a homage to its previous life.

The Order of St Clare advocated extreme poverty and separation, but the York nuns were slightly more open than the norm. They hosted a documentary about the convent in the 1960s, giving insights into their daily routine of 5am prayers, chores, meditation and 8pm bedtime (probably slightly different to the routine going on there now). They were also famous for their Rhubarb Wine, made from the rhubarb grown in the convent's vegetable patches and sold at local fairs.

The monastery continued until 2013 when the large building and five acres of ground became a bit too much for the declining order – by this point there were only eight nuns left. It was empty for a few years until Vita York decided to purchase the land and build premier student accommodation around the historically protected buildings. Objects relating to the leisure and work activities of the nuns have been incorporated into the interior design, so you still get a sense of the history of the place. Old tennis rackets and croquet mallets hang on the walls of the games room, pieces of a domino set were made into a clock, and the nuns' sewing machines are on display in one of the study rooms. The old chapel is undoubtedly the most impressive room in the complex: the designers preserved the pew-seats along the walls, added old bells to the décor and kept the original stained-glass window to let in the light.

THE DRAGON STONES

York's miniature version of Stonehenge

St Nicholas Nature Reserve
Rawdon Avenue, YO10 3FW

In the middle of St Nicholas Nature Reserve is a curious monument. Made from the fragments of an old church, the Dragon Stones are York's miniature version of Stonehenge. The story of how this wonder appeared is slightly less mysterious than the real Stonehenge, however: they were put up by a group of local actors in 1995 as part of an open-air theatre set.

Before becoming a henge and a venue, these church stones were just some of many discarded objects and materials that were scattered around the site. Although St Nicholas Nature Reserve is now the green heart of the city, for years this land was the dumping ground of York's domestic and industrial waste. The land was originally home to the City Corporation's brick works site, but when brick production stopped in the 1950s another purpose had to be found for the empty pits and kilns that were left behind. The York Corporation Civic Amenity Tip and Landfill Organisation found a new purpose for them, namely as disposal containers for the waste, asbestos and metal of the city. The tip became an unbearable rubbish pile and was eventually closed in the 1970s following a local petition, and nature started to return to the area.

Fifty years later, St Nick's is an environmentalist's dream. It became an official nature reserve in the 1990s and was placed under the stewardship of the newly registered charity Friends of St Nicholas Fields. As part of this project, clay was spread over the area to form walking paths, and thousands of trees, shrubs and flowers were planted by local volunteers. These initiatives have supported a biodiversity programme that has led to almost 1,000 species being discovered in St Nick's woodlands today: species are typically found through the weekly organised nature walks that are attended by a team of loyal followers.

INNER SPACE STATION SERVICE STATION

Last shop before Mars

339 Hull Road, YO10 3LE

On the way up Hull Road, towards the A64, a strange outline of a man standing on top of a petrol station starts to appear on the horizon. As you get closer, it becomes clear that the man is not a man at all – he is a Cyberman, standing on top of the family-run Inner Space Station Service Station, a spot on the way into or out of the city where you can fill up or snack down. With the novelty toys and the themed décor, if you are in need of fuel, refreshments, or a car wash, it will be tough finding a more interesting place to go than this.

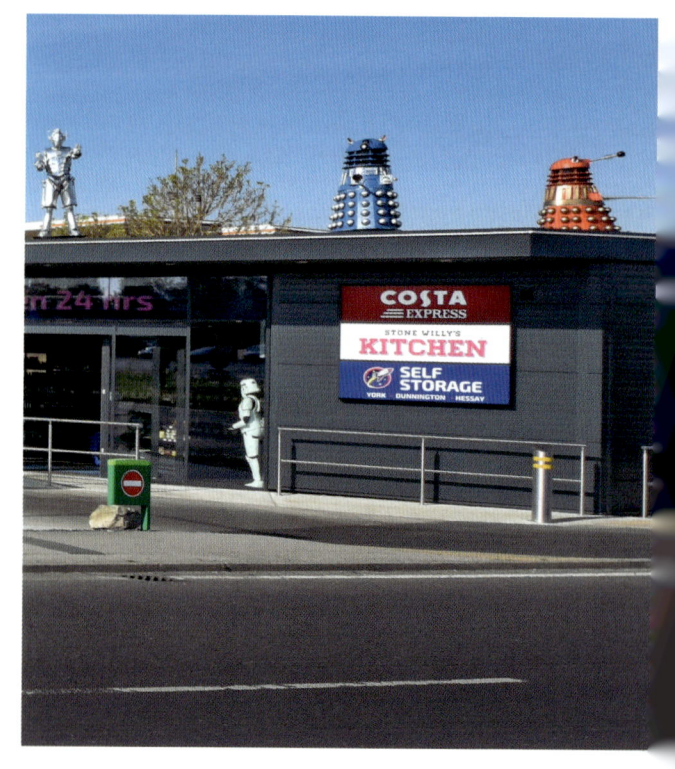

Established in the 1990s, this wacky service station is an example of an independent fuel business, where owners form partnerships with leading oil companies in order to receive their fuel but where they can do whatever they want with the general site. This flexibility gave owner Graham Kennedy an opportunity to live out his dream of owning an intergalactic space station – it is the first step in preparing for a future that sees us all buying our fuel in space.

The space-locals that decorate the station consist of three Daleks, one Cyberman, one Tardis (from *Doctor Who*, now protecting the roof of the services), one Boba Fett (a character from *Star Wars*, Bobda Fett was the bounty hunter who captured Hans Solo and now provides security for the ATM) and four Transformers.

They have travelled from all over the world to feature in this eclectic mix of sci-fi characters: some were made by local Harrogate theatre set designers, and some from sci-fi model creators in Thailand.

A recent redevelopment and complete interior design makeover means that the station has now fully embraced the space theme. There were even rumours of a full-sized flying saucer to be featured in the décor, but this plan has been pushed back for the time being.

Inner Space Stations. York.

THE TOMB OF MARY WARD

㉚

When a Protestant priest accepted a bribe in exchange for finding a space for a Catholic nun ...

St Thomas's Church
Osbaldwick Lane, YO10 3DB
osbaldwickandmurtonchurches.org.uk
Daily 9am–5pm

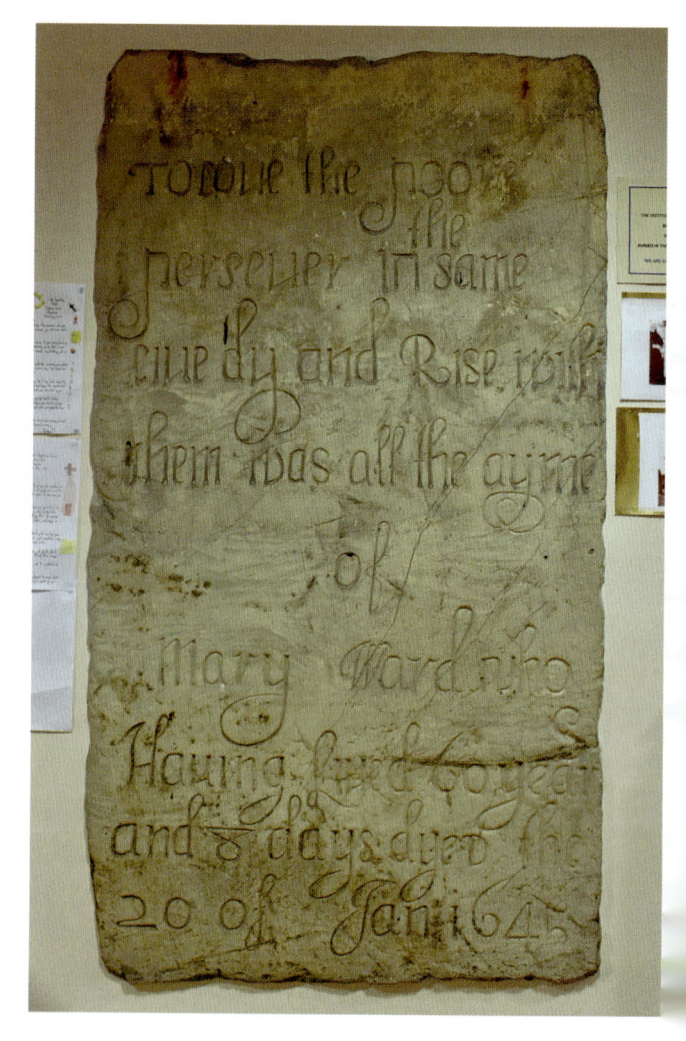

Sister Mary Ward is about as famous as Catholic nuns get. By spending her whole life teaching religious tolerance and female activism, she has been immortalised in the names of countless schools and churches across the world. Yet despite her international reputation, her body was secretly buried in the unknown church of St Thomas in the tiny village of Osbaldwick. She has been so well revered that any renovation to the church was organised around the location of her tombstone – the huge stone slab is now built into the wall with the inscription facing outwards for all to see.

Sister Ward lived in England at a time when Catholicism was punishable by death. Born in Yorkshire in 1585, she grew up holding deeply religious beliefs and progressive ideas about women, which eventually made her a controversial figure for both Protestants and Catholics. She passionately believed that 'women in time will come to do much' and she stubbornly spent her life proving that they could. Ignoring the religious conventions which stated that female Catholics should stay behind the walls of convents, she set up secret schools for Catholic women across Europe, journeyed on foot over the Alps (not once but twice) and even won an argument with the pope himself.

Because of her blatant disregard for the confining rules of her religious leaders, Mary Ward was imprisoned by the Catholic Inquisition under the accusation of heresy. But it seems she was a force to be reckoned with and she was eventually released by the pope. She was allowed to carry on with her active religious service, going on to establish the religious order of the Congregation of Jesus.

She continued to practise the prohibited religion in her home country, and when she died at the age of 60, St Thomas's remote location seemed the perfect place to entomb her. Being Catholic, there were not many places she could be buried legally, but luckily the Protestant priest at St Thomas's was pragmatic enough to accept a bribe in exchange for finding a space in the churchyard for her. Although the tombstone now takes pride of place in the church, no one knows the exact location in the graveyard where her bones lie, except the priest that buried her, about 400 years ago.

THE DERWENT VALLEY LIGHT RAILWAY

The Blackberry Line

Murton Lane, YO19 5UF
murtonpark.co.uk
Every Sunday passengers can take a short train ride on the remaining section of the Derwent Light Valley Railway on the weekly volunteer-run experience
See website for opening times and admission prices

Alongside the tractors and agricultural equipment held at Murton Park's Museum of Farming, there is also a fully restored, fully operational, Edwardian train station. Far out of town, this is York's unknown railway, vastly overshadowed by the grand Victorian central station. The Derwent Valley Light Railway is now a half-mile heritage train track run by volunteers, but it was originally designed to carry agricultural produce in and out of the city centre. Lovingly referred to as the 'Blackberry Line', the carriages were filled with fruits and vegetables from the outlying districts and taken into York for the local markets.

From 1913 the railway also ran a public passenger service, offering the citizens of York the opportunity of venturing out into the clean air of the Yorkshire countryside for a spot of blackberry picking. The train ran as a private operation for many years and even managed to avoid being nationalised with the rest of the country's railway system during the post-war period. It was used for agricultural products but as demand for local produce fell, the tracks were sold off or dismantled piece by piece, leaving only a small section of unused railway remaining.

The tiny station building, which now stands next to the track, came to Murton Park in the 1990s. Originally located in Wheldrake, which was about six miles away along the Derwent Valley Light Railway track, the station had stood empty and unused for a few decades following the closure of that part of the line. Each piece of the station was carefully disassembled and transported to Murton. The structure was then rebuilt next to the Murton train tracks and returned to a wonderfully nostalgic operational railway station. There are even plans to connect the little station to the city centre with new railway tracks, so one day it will be an entirely functioning railway station. The train, the tracks and the station all fit into Murton Park's atmosphere of romantic escape. They take visitors back to a time of local produce from local farming and the days of tiny trains filled with blackberries.

ALPHABETICAL INDEX

Acomb Wood and Meadow Local Nature Reserve	190
Aerodrome Memorial	132
All Saints Church	128
Anglian Tower	20
Arup building	76
Askham Bog	192
Bachelor Hill	188
Baile Hill	164
Bedern Hall	62
Bell ringing at York Oratory	30
'Best British Roundabout'	183
Bettys' mirror	122
Biggest duck ever to have lived	215
Bile Beans	144
Bishophill Community Garden	88
Bitchdaughter Tower	165
Boot scrapers	29
Bootham Park Hospital	148
Bootham School Assembly Hall	149
Boundary stones	26
Bright Victorians	125
Cat sculptures	92
Ceiling of the York Art Gallery	14
Ceremony Room of York Lodge 236	36
Chaplin House staircase	91
Chapter House roof	56
Cholera Burial Ground	82
Clay Pipe at the Black Swan Inn	106
Coffin drop of the Golden Slipper Pub	64
Cold War bunker	180
Column of the George Inn	120
Comic carvings	87
Competition of angles	31
Council Chamber	118
Crossed keys of Dean Court Hotel	32
Derwent Valley Light Railway	230
Destructor	142
Dick Turpin's fake grave	100
Disappearing railway lines	206
Doors of the York Grand Hotel basement	81
Dragon Stones	224
Drinking fountain in Museum Gardens	22
Dryad sculpture	215
Dutch House	67

Face of a stonemason	61
Famous Chocolate Orange was once an apple	203
Fire insurance plaques	46
First female jockey	201
First modern lesbian	16
Flood board	172
Former Electrobus Station	150
Fossgate Barrier	173
From green to red ...	35
Game	165
George Leeman statue	80
Glass case of an old slipper	65
Guildhall	119
Half a cat	93
Half-smoked angel of All Saints Church	85
Hanging wooden Bible	42
Haxby Road footpath	138
Henry Richardson's memorial	166
Heslington Hall and gardens	214
Historic street signs	27
Holgate Windmill	182
Holy Trinity Church	60
Ice house	14.
Infamous alumni	15.
Inner Space Station service station	226
Inscription of the Ancient Society of Florists	11
Inscription of the Waterfront House Bakery	17
Jacob's Well	8
Jewbury plaque	7
John Snow's pump	8
Joseph Rowntree Theatre	13
Kohima Museum	21
Lady Anne's effigy	9
Lady Peckett's Yard	10
Liberty police office	5
Long line of 'blue bridges'	17
Manhole cover with pulleys	14
Mansion House cat	1.
Mason's loft	8
Memorial library	1
Merchant Taylors' Hall	6
Minute memories	2
Model of the Chapter House roof	

- 232 -

More plague stones in York	197	Snuffer on the Red House Antiques Centre	28
Morrell Yard	104	Solar System cycle path	194
Mouse on St William's College	65	St Aidan's Church	187
Nails of the statue of Edward II	50	St Andrew's Drill Hall	112
New Earswick	130	St Anthony's garden	72
Norman tower	220	St Mary's Tower	155
North Eastern Railway War Memorial	78	St Olave's churchyard	156
Nose of Queen Victoria's statue	184	St Paul's Square	160
Nunnery Wall	168	Statue of a Native American	48
Old Palace Library and Archive	58	Statue of Terry's Chocolate Orange	202
Other snuffers in York	29	Statues of Bootham Bar	18
Peace Garden	146	Stone house	44
Pikeing Well	208	Sunset walk at York Racecourse	200
Plague stone	196	Taxidermy of an English Shepherd	97
Plaque of the grave of Joseph Rowntree	212	Tether rings	129
		The Big Blue Pipe sculpture	140
Poppleton Railway Nursery	178	Tomb of Mary Ward	228
Priests' hole of the secret chapel	162	Tyburn stone	198
Prisoners' signatures	96	Unique 100% English chocolate	139
Protected Odeon sign	163	Unitarian Chapel	108
Public vegetable bed	174	University of York Lake	216
Raindale Mill	98	Vast teapot collection	123
Reception of St Peter's School	152	View behind the Multangular Tower	24
Ridge and furrow	197	Viking church	157
Rocket in the Hiscox building	110	Vita York	222
Roman Bath Museum	114	War of the breweries	67
Roman rock	135	Where do the names Swinegate and Grape Lane come from?	117
Roman wall of Bootham Bar	19		
Rowntree Park Reading Café	205	White Row	186
Royal Mail postbox stamp	34	Women in the fraternity	37
Search Engine	158	Wooden shutters	151
Severus Water Tower	189	Yearsley Swimming Pool's inscription	134
Shameless officers	207	York Cat Trail map	93
Sign of the gateway to Roman fortress	66	York Conservation Trust	105
Signed bricks	116	York Drill and Army Museum	94
Siren sculpture	49	York Medical Society Museum	38
Siward's Howe burial ground	219	York Philosophical Society Library	23
Siward's Howe Water Tower	218	York 'zero' post	159
Sneak holes of All Saints Church	84		

NOTES

NOTES

ABOUT JONGLEZ PUBLISHING

It was September 1995 and Thomas Jonglez was in Peshawar, the northern Pakistani city 20 kilometres from the tribal zone he was to visit a few days later. It occurred to him that he should record the hidden aspects of his native city, Paris, which he knew so well. During his seven-month trip back home from Beijing, the countries he crossed took in Tibet (entering clandestinely, hidden under blankets in an overnight bus), Iran and Kurdistan. He never took a plane but travelled by boat, train or bus, hitchhiking, cycling, on horseback or on foot, reaching Paris just in time to celebrate Christmas with the family.

On his return, he spent two fantastic years wandering the streets of the capital to gather material for his first "secret guide", written with a friend. For the next seven years he worked in the steel industry until the passion for discovery overtook him. He launched Jonglez Publishing in 2003 and moved to Venice three years later.

In 2013, in search of new adventures, the family left Venice and spent six months travelling to Brazil, via North Korea, Micronesia, the Solomon Islands, Easter Island, Peru and Bolivia.

After seven years in Rio de Janeiro, he now lives in Berlin with his wife and three children.

Jonglez Publishing produces a range of titles in nine languages, released in 40 countries.

FROM THE SAME PUBLISHER

ATLASES

Atlas of extreme weather
Atlas of forbidden places
Atlas of geographical curiosities
Atlas of unusual wines

PHOTO BOOKS

Abandoned America
Abandoned Asylums
Abandoned Australia
Abandoned Belgium
Abandoned Churches: Unclaimed places of worship
Abandoned cinemas of the world
Abandoned France
Abandoned Germany
Abandoned Italy
Abandoned Japan
Abandoned Lebanon
Abandoned Spain
Abandoned USSR
Abandoned world – An AI-generated exploration
After the Final Curtain – The Fall of the American Movie Theater
After the Final Curtain – America's Abandoned Theaters
Baikonur – Vestiges of the Soviet space programme
Cinemas – A French heritage
Clickbait – A visual journey through AI-generated stories
Forbidden France
Forbidden Places – Vol. 1
Forbidden Places – Vol. 2
Forbidden Places – Vol. 3
Forgotten France
Forgotten Heritage
Oblivion
Secret sacred sites
Venice deserted
Venice from the skies

'SOUL OF' GUIDES

Soul of Athens
Soul of Barcelona
Soul of Berlin
Soul of Brussels
Soul of Kyoto
Soul of Lisbon
Soul of Los Angeles
Soul of Marrakesh
Soul of Marseille
Soul of Milan
Soul of New York
Soul of Rome
Soul of Tokyo
Soul of Venice

'SECRET' GUIDES

Secret Amsterdam
Secret Bali – An unusual guide
Secret Bangkok
Secret Barcelona
Secret Bath – An unusual guide
Secret Belfast
Secret Berlin
Secret Boston – An unusual guide
Secret Brighton – An unusual guide
Secret Brooklyn – An unusual guide
Secret Brussels
Secret Budapest
Secret Buenos Aires
Secret Campania
Secret Cape Town
Secret Copenhagen
Secret Dolomites
Secret Dublin – An unusual guide
Secret Edinburgh – An unusual guide
Secret Florence
Secret French Riviera
Secret Geneva
Secret Glasgow
Secret Granada
Secret Helsinki
Secret Istanbul
Secret Johannesburg
Secret Lisbon
Secret Liverpool – An unusual guide
Secret London – An unusual guide
Secret London – Unusual bars & restaurants
Secret Los Angeles – An unusual guide
Secret Louisiana – An unusual guide
Secret Madrid
Secret Mexico City
Secret Milan
Secret Montreal – An unusual guide
Secret Naples
Secret New Orleans – An unusual guide
Secret New York – An unusual guide
Secret New York – Curious activities
Secret New York – Hidden bars & restaurants
Secret Normandy
Secret Paris
Secret Potsdam
Secret Prague
Secret Provence
Secret Rio de Janeiro
Secret Rome
Secret Seville
Secret Singapore
Secret Sussex – An unusual guide
Secret Tokyo
Secret Tuscany
Secret Venice

Follow us on Facebook and Instagram

ACKNOWLEDGEMENTS

Thanks to Simon Luck, Clive Goodhead, Susie Young, Graham Mitchell, Catherine Hodgson, Steve Heraty-Wells, Robert Scott, David Hull, Jacqueline Ward, Mike Curley, Jane Mortimer, Eleanor Davies, Mardi Jacobs, Graham Harries, John Galvin, Ed Van der Molen, Roger Lee, Graham Wilford, Andrew Hill, Odelia Cheung, Alex Brown, Graham Kennedy, Debbie Milliner, Craig Benton, Simon Baylis, Joshua Chapman, Ann Stafford, Explore York, the church wardens of St Olaves, Keith Crowther and the team at Jonglez Publishing.

And above all thank you to Chris Akerman and Katy Berry for their constant support in all my escapades, and for having all the good ideas but never taking any of the credit.

PHOTOGRAPHY CREDITS

All photographs were taken by Isobel Akerman with the exception of:
York Art Gallery ceiling in re-construction: Peter Heaton
Inner Space tation service station: Copyright Inner Space Service Station. York
The Black Swan back room: Wikimedia Malcolmxl5
Historic picture of the Arup building: Reproduced from an original held by City of York Council/ Explore Libraries and Archives Mutual, York [Image y9_rou_5255_b]
Historic picture of St Lawrence Church: Reproduced from an original held by City of York Council/ Explore Libraries and Archives Mutual, York. Image y1_stlaw_2179
Terry's Chocolate Orange Box: Copyright York Museums Trust (York Castle Museum)
Bile Beans: Advert: Medically approved Bile Beans. Wellcome Collection

Maps: Cyrille Suss – **Layout:** Emmanuelle Willard Toulemonde – **Copy-editing:** Sigrid Newman – **Proofreading:** Nikki Shanahan – **Publishing:** Clémence Mathé

In accordance with regularly upheld French jurisprudence (Toulouse 14-01-1887), the publisher will not be deemed responsible for any involuntary errors or omissions that may subsist in this guide despite our diligence and verifications by the editorial staff.
Any reproduction of the content, or part of the content, of this book by whatever means is forbidden without prior authorisation by the publisher.

© JONGLEZ 2025
Registration of copyright: March 2025 – Edition: 02
ISBN: 978-2-36195-767-4
Printed in Bulgaria by Dedrax